ON THE FRONT PORCH IN LOUISIANA

The Garcia Family Witnesses 100 Years Of Louisiana History

DANIEL F. OPPLIGER

Printed in the United States of America

First Printing Edition, 2024

ISBN 979-8-218-98316-1

Dedication

Dedicated to Adele Garcia Haley, my grandmother, who used to share stories about her family, and to Edith Garcia O'Dell, who added valuable insights.

Contents

Author's Note

This book has been a lifelong endeavor of mine. During my graduate studies, I undertook a library science course aimed at responding punctually to physicians' inquiries. This training laid the groundwork for accumulating three boxes of family records. Initially, these archives yielded little information, with many letters marked "no information available." However, the advent of the internet brought a wealth of new sources. Historical newspapers and Google Books emerged as invaluable resources in piecing together the pieces of our family history.

When I sought records from the Missouri Medical College, I was cautioned that information on Charles Garcia might be scarce. However, the archives of the Franciscan Sisters of Mary revealed files documenting the care of 930 patients by Dr. Garcia. St. Louis newspapers also provided extensive coverage beyond what is detailed in this book.

This endeavor has been greatly aided by the support and contributions of several individuals: Richard Ames, Dr. Paul Anderson, Marlene Darensbourg, Rita Frampton, Adele Garcia Haley, Mary Huxhold, Jerry Gandolfo, John Adrian Garcia, Renee Garcia, Marcella Jost, Barbara Munson, Duane Montz, Edith Garcia

O'Dell, Ashley Rogers, Jay Schexnaydre, John W Skardon, Sister Marylu Stueber, Careen Valentine, and Charles Elliott Wayne (formerly Charles Wayne Garcia).

The Archdiocese of New Orleans served as a vital source for baptism and marriage records, while the Franciscan Sisters of Mary Archives preserved Dr. Charles Garcia's medical history. Google Books uncovered details about Felix's activities in Paris. The Jack D.L. Holmes collection at the University of West Florida, Pensacola, chronicled most of Manuel Garcia Y Muniz's career. Despite efforts, the Spanish archives in Havana yielded minimal information through a hired researcher.

Local repositories such as the New Orleans Public Library and the Notarial Archives of New Orleans provided maps, property transactions, probate records, and other documents essential to reconstructing family history. The St. Charles Borromeo Parish Archives offer insights into property and slave records alongside notable events linked to Widow Massicot's property. Similarly, the St. John the Baptist Parish Archives provided further property records.

At Tulane University Special Collections, extensive documentation referenced the Garcia family, primarily sourced from the New Orleans Times-Picayune newspapers. Likewise, the University of Texas-Austin housed copies of the Ft. Worth Telegram, offering additional perspectives. Resources like Genealogy Bank and ProQuest Historical Newspapers contributed to uncovering broader historical contexts integral to understanding the Garcia family's legacy.

Interestingly, Bill Oppliger, my father, renovated St. John the Baptist Parish church in the 1980s. The renovation included decorative painting, deep cleaning and updates in fixtures, lighting, etc. Bill was working for Conrad Schmidt Studios of Milwaukee, WI, at the time. He had no idea he was working on my mother's ancestral church. One day, he was invited to the rectory after hours for Maker's Mark. The priest said, "Nothing but the finest for God's servants."

Introduction

The Garcia family's roots in New Orleans trace back to the early years following the Spanish acquisition of Louisiana. Manuel Garcia y Muniz, a native of Puerto Real, Andalucía, stands as my fourth great-grandfather. His presence marks the beginning of a tale intertwined with Louisiana's formative history. His sons - Felix, Manuel, and Carlos - played pivotal roles in the early political and military development of the state. (J. D. Holmes, Dramatis Personae 1965)

Felix notably served as President of the Louisiana Senate from 1840 to 1852, yet historical accounts of his tenure remain sparse. This book highlights key legislative milestones, bypassing exhaustive detail. Little is documented about the Crescent Regiment, where Charles, Felix's son, served under General Beauregard. The narrative traces their journey from formation through meetings to Shiloh, culminating in a remarkable incident involving General Bragg, widely reported in over 20 newspapers at the time. Post-war, Charles ventured to St. Louis, where he transformed a modest sum of 40 cents into a considerable fortune.

In Louisiana, plantations operated as businesses, with only a few featuring the grand houses often romanticized in movies. Charles Garcia's birth record remains elusive, leading us to draw reasonable conclusions from family history, notes, and photographs. His mother hailed from Alsace, France, and family lore indicates his grandmother resided in Paris, with Madeleine Adrian being a revered name passed down through generations.

The Garcia surname, pronounced "Gar-sha" in our family, holds significant meaning. Insights from Adele and Edith, both Garcia by birth, provided the foundational narratives. My aunt Marilyn's recollection hints at the family's affluence, a sentiment echoed by my mother's belief in their origins from Salamanca.

Join this exploration of the Garcia family saga - a story brimming with political influence, military service, entrepreneurial success, and the pursuit of uncovering the past.

Chapter One:
Roots In Spain

Like mighty trees, families branch out through generations, their roots anchoring them in the fertile soil of history. Each individual life, a unique leaf, contributes to the overall story, shaping the narrative and influencing the branches that follow. The Garcias' family saga is no different. It begins not with a grand historical event but with a single individual, and his origins were not in the lively streets of New Orleans but under the warm sun of Spain. Generations ago, the family tree took root, its branches reaching across the centuries to connect to the present day. The true spark of Garcia's history ignites with the arrival of Manuel Garcia y Muniz, a man whose spirit burned as brightly as his ambition and sense of adventure.

Manuel Garcia y Muniz left a lasting impression on all who encountered him. He was often described as someone who possessed a distinctly Spanish air. He seemed to exist outside his time, a century ahead of his peers.

Upon first glance, one couldn't help but notice his desperate need for a haircut. Tall and angular, his long, flowing black hair cascaded down his back, reminiscent of the famed Don Quixote. Perhaps, like Cervantes' hero, Manuel harbored a touch of absurd romanticism and chivalrous spirit. His hair, though undeniably black, sported an unusual style. It seems his barber, not content with simply taming his mane, fashioned it into a pompadour, complete with a slight curl at the ends. (Garcia 1954)

His attire was a fascinating mix. A neatly folded white silk muffler adorned his neck, contrasting with a crisp white vest. Black stock encircled his neck, not constricting, but just enough to frame his white cravat, which, like a pirate's beard, completely covered the middle portion of the stock. His eyes were large and fierce, hinting at the bravado of Long John Silver himself. They were the kind that would ignite a child's imagination about real pirates. His face, captured in a semi-profile, showed Mr. Garcia y Muniz peering out from the corner of his eyes, a hint of a sinister yet debonair expression playing on his lips. One could almost hear the swagger of a pirate captain, even if slightly unearned.

While his wide, weathered face, reminiscent of a seasoned buccaneer, might have possessed a few flaws – his nose, for instance, being both exceptionally long and prominently hooked – it retained an undeniable nobility in profile. This noble aquiline line, he seemed determined to preserve. But the most telling feature, as with any human, was his mouth. Hidden behind a formidable mustache and beard, it was as if Manuel sought to shield his true character from scrutiny. (Garcia 1954)

Manuel Garcia y Muniz from a collection of Virginia May Seay Garcia.

Hailing from Puerto Real, Spain, Manuel Garcia y Muniz was born in 1765 (J. D. Holmes 1965). The son of Juan Antonio Garcia and Francisca Xaviela Muniz of Salamanca, his early years in Spain remain shrouded in the mists of time. However, driven by an unknown yearning, he set sail across the vast Atlantic in the early 1790s from Puerto Real, his compass pointed towards the vibrant, cosmopolitan city of New Orleans. Little is known about his initial steps on

American soil. However, the burgeoning port city, packed with diverse cultures and languages, must have starkly contrasted his Spanish roots. With his inherent resourcefulness and adaptability, Manuel carved a niche for himself in this new world. He found his calling on the mighty Mississippi River, navigating its treacherous currents and ever-shifting sandbars as a skilled riverboat pilot.

However, Manuel's ambitions extended beyond the helm of a riverboat. He possessed a keen intellect, a thirst for adventure, and a natural leadership quality. These qualities, coupled with his unwavering dedication, propelled him towards a remarkable rise in the ranks of the Louisiana militia. Recognized for his courage and strategic thinking, Manuel was entrusted with the responsibility of safeguarding the fledgling colony. On October 5th, 1793, he received a distinguished appointment as a lieutenant in the Louisiana militia, his provisional salary reflecting the value placed on his skills. He quickly rose through the ranks, starting as second-in-command of the Squadron of Galleys patrolling the Mississippi River.

His leadership potential was evident, and by April 15th, 1796, he found himself promoted to commander. This rapid ascension culminated in two significant milestones on March 29th, 1796: a royal appointment confirming his lieutenancy and a promotion to captaincy in the regular army.

Garcia's service record was nothing short of impressive. He played a vital role in protecting Louisiana during the war with France (1794-1795) by commanding a division of galleys at Fort San Felipe de Placaminas, a strategic location guarding the Mississippi River south of New Orleans. He even ventured further afield, crossing the Gulf of Mexico aboard the warship "La Fina" during this period. His contributions extended beyond wartime duties. In February 1795,

Garcia's expertise and leadership were called upon for a crucial mission. He volunteered as an engineer and second-in-command of the galleys, joining Governor Gayoso and Captain Pedro Rousseau on an expedition that would establish a significant Spanish presence in the region. (J. D. Holmes, Dramatis Peronae 1965)

It took 55 days to travel upstream from New Orleans to Barrancas. This journey was accomplished using poles and flat bottom boats. During this time, repairs were made to the damaged ships. Unfortunately, La Activa encountered an accident that rendered it out of service. However, La Flecha was eventually repaired and successfully reached Barrancas on May 19th. Additionally, La Venganza, repaired in New Orleans and loaded with supplies and annual presents for the Arkansas and Chickasaw Indians, sailed upriver, made its deliveries, and arrived at Barrancas on June 12th. Upon arrival, García discovered that most of the squadron's vessels were already present, including the galleys La Luisiana, La Victoria, and La Felipa, the galiot La Flecha, and the cañonera El Rayo. Considering that the fleet was to be based in Barrancas for the rest of the year, García established his permanent headquarters for the naval forces on the Island of Fooy. (Nasatir 1968)

This expedition resulted in the founding of San Fernando de las Barrancas, a Spanish post strategically located on the Chickasaw Bluffs (present-day Memphis, Tennessee.) Garcia remained instrumental in the development and defense of this post until its evacuation and destruction in March 1797. He then played a role in the construction of a new post, aptly named Esperanza (later known as Hopefield, Arkansas), situated strategically across the Mississippi River from the former Chickasaw Bluffs.

As his military career flourished, Manuel established himself as a prominent figure in New Orleans society. He found love and built a family, marrying into a respected Massicot family. This union not only solidified his position within the community but also marked the beginning of his journey as a landowner, acquiring properties that would become a cornerstone of the Garcia family legacy.

In the 1790s, he met Aimée Massicot, the one who finally brought his love ship to harbor. The heavens smiled upon their union. In the name of the Holy Family, the marriage contract was signed. Don Manuel Garcia, a native of Puerto Real de Andalucia, and Dona Aimée Massicot, daughter of the esteemed Captain Jacques B. Massicot (Massicot later became Judge of St. Charles Parish) and his wife, Dame Genovena Grevenbourg (late known as Widow Massicot) of New Orleans, were bound together in holy matrimony. The year was 1790, the month of November, and the setting was the vibrant city of New Orleans.

This sacred union was not just a matter of love, but also a strategic alliance. To solidify the bond, Manuel, in accordance with the customs of the time, offered his wife a dowry. This dowry included various possessions, each listed in an official document. (Ximenez 1790)

The list comprised a plot of land on Bourbon Street at St. Peter, bordering the property of Joseph Hernandez. This modest plot, measuring thirty square meters, held a value of five hundred pesos. The dowry extended beyond mere land. It also included a young black woman named Amanda, a Creole of twenty-four years, described as "de Venegad." Her estimated value was four hundred pesos. Another woman, Amanda Delachi, was also part of the dowry. She was adopted from the Nuger family the previous year, and she was valued at four hundred pesos as well. Various household items, including silverware and a bed alone, valued at twenty-four pesos, were also in the dowry. The total value of all the gifts amounted to one thousand one hundred and fifty pesos.

Manuel emphasized that those possessions were hers to keep, even in the event of his death, divorce, or any other unforeseen circumstance. He declared his intention to uphold this agreement and vowed not to use these items to settle any future debts or personal transgressions. He further asserted his commitment to honoring his wife's rights and those of any future heirs. With this exchange, not just a marriage but a new chapter in both their lives was officially sealed.

Manuel Garcia y Muniz, a man as multifaceted as the city he called home, stood at a crossroads. Having carved a name for himself on land and water, his future held the promise of love, family, and the potential to leave a lasting mark on a burgeoning city. However, even within the confines of his new life, a spark of his adventurous spirit lingered, waiting to be rekindled by the challenges and triumphs that would lie ahead.

Chapter Two:
Struggles And Triumphs

The winds of change swept across the late 18th and early 19th centuries, shaping the lives of Manuel Garcia y Muñiz and his family. Life in those times was harsh. Many children succumbed to illness before reaching adulthood due to limited access to proper medical care. Manuel and his wife, Aimée Luce Massicot, were not spared this reality. Their firstborn, Manuel Joseph Luis De Santa Maria Garcia II, arrived in 1795, followed by Felix Juan De Dios Garcia in 1803. The youngest son, Carlos Garcia, was born around 1806. Felix and Carlos received their education at the Spanish fort in Pensacola, with Felix venturing into the field of science and Carlos pursuing a career in law. All the children received the sacrament of baptism at St. Louis Cathedral in New Orleans. (Orleans 1803)

Manuel and Aimée also had four daughters. Their eldest daughter, Candida Bibiana Garcia, married Lieutenant Luis Daunoy y Macarty in 1809 in Pensacola, FL, uniting the Garcia family with prominent figures in Louisiana and West Florida. (Ames 2015) The couple welcomed three more daughters: Aimée Euphrosie Garcia (born around 1797) and Josephine Garcia, who married Alexander Baldwin, and Rosalie.

While family life presented its challenges, Manuel Garcia actively served his community. He rose to the rank of Lieutenant Colonel in the Spanish Coast Guard. As a Lieutenant Colonel, he was tasked with the crucial responsibility of curbing smuggling activities. At the time, it was a rampant issue that plagued the region. Nicknamed the "spy among spies," his role involved monitoring the infamous Lafitte brothers who were notorious smugglers operating in Louisiana. (Guadeloupe Privateers in Barataria 1969)

He rose to the position as his talents caught the eye of the Spanish governor, Carondelet. Initially, he recognized Garcia's potential and appointed him second-in-command of the river squadron in 1793. Despite his official promotion, Garcia wouldn't be formally assigned to the squadron until 1795. Prior to that, he served under Carondelet's command in 1794, stationed at Placaminas with the galley La Leal, where he was tasked with guarding the Mississippi's mouth.

His career, however, wasn't without its share of complications. In 1795, while commanding La Fina, Garcia found himself embroiled in a conflict with Benjamin Fooy, who was an interpreter and Indian agent. A misunderstanding arose, possibly due to language barriers, and it resulted in a heated exchange that led to Garcia's arrest. He was confined aboard La Castilla for nearly three months.

This incident displayed a stubborn streak in Garcia's personality. Despite the temporary setback, his commitment to his duties wasn't significantly affected. When illness forced the squadron's commander, Rousseau, to retire in 1796, Garcia stepped up to fill the vacancy. His leadership qualities were recognized by Carondelet, who recommended Garcia for a promotion to Lieutenant in the army in acknowledgement of his efforts against French privateers. Garcia's bravery extended beyond the Mississippi. He actively patrolled the Gulf of Mexico, keeping a watchful eye on American activities and even engaging the British brigantine Hero in combat. (J. D. Holmes, Dramatis Peronae 1965)

Buoyed by this recognition, Garcia embarked on his next mission – navigating the Mississippi River alongside Lieutenant Colonel Carlos Howard. Lieutenant Colonel Carlos Howard proved to be a valuable companion for Garcia. Together, they navigated the Mississippi in close proximity to an American expeditionary force led by Captain Isaac Guion. It was a tense situation that lasted until they reached the Spanish post of Nogales (present-day Vicksburg). Garcia remained stationed there until February 1798.

His next mission involved leading a squadron of warships down the Mississippi River to the Balize delta, where three English privateer ships were blockading the river's mouth and posing a threat to the pilot station. Garcia's decisive actions disrupted their plans. In September 1799, he boldly engaged an English brigantine, the Hero, which had been preventing commercial vessels from entering the Mississippi.

Garcia's commitment continued when the notorious adventurer, William Augustus Bowles, re-emerged in West Florida, causing trouble for the Spanish authorities. Bowles' audacity even extended to recapturing Fort San Marcos de Apalache in 1800. In response, Garcia was entrusted with the command of three galleys and two armed launches. His objective was to patrol the coast and intercept Bowles if possible.

Success followed Garcia. He managed to capture Bowles' aide-de-camp along with several associates. Furthermore, on April 1, 1800, Garcia's forces seized the English warship Gavilan - a vessel armed with eight cannons and carrying ammunition and supplies intended for Bowles' allies, the Seminole tribe.

In June 1800, Garcia played a pivotal role in the Spanish counteroffensive. Following orders from Governor Folch of Pensacola, he organized the ships and led the recapture of Fort San Marcos. His strategic maneuvers on June 23rd pressured the enemy, ultimately leading to their retreat. The following day, Garcia's forces captured a flag and three of Bowles' boats loaded with supplies and ammunition.

These accomplishments earned Garcia a well-deserved promotion. His provisional captain's rank was solidified, and he was officially recognized as a Captain on October 20, 1802. His service continued throughout the year, as he conducted two vital convoys from New Orleans to the Apalache post and participated in blockading the area to prevent potential resupply efforts from Bowles' supporters based in Nassau. (J. D. Holmes, Pensacola Settlers, 1781-1821 1970)

While his military career was filled with action and the defense of Spanish interests, Manuel Garcia also dabbled in land acquisition. In 1806, he secured a sizable piece of real estate – 15,000 arpents along the Mississippi River in Feliciana.

In 1804, Manuel Garcia found a glimmer of hope in his pursuit of land ownership. Vicente Sebastian Pintado, an authorized surveyor, played a crucial role by measuring and marking the boundaries of a substantial 15,000 arpents of land in Garcia's favor. Pintado's official documentation, providing details on the land's location and neighboring areas, solidified Garcia's claim. This surveying act became a vital piece of evidence in the ensuing legal battle that unfolded.

In September 1806, Manuel Garcia took a significant step towards land acquisition. He purchased a substantial plot of 15,000 arpents from the Spanish government in the newly formed region of St. Helena, located in Feliciana Parish, present-day Louisiana. This transaction marked a turning point in Garcia's life, potentially securing his future or expanding his ventures. Little did he know these events had set the stage for a prolonged legal dispute, where Pintado's surveying would become crucial evidence.

After Manuel Garcia's hopeful pursuit of land ownership, the situation took a turn. A law passed by the United States Congress in 1804 complicated matters. This law stated that any land grants made by the Spanish government in West Florida after 1801 were no longer valid. This created a problem for those who had bought land from the Spanish government in good faith. The affected area included parts of present-day Louisiana, Mississippi, and Alabama. However, negotiations between the United States and Spain began in 1818 for the transfer of the Floridas to the United States. This brought a ray of hope for those affected by the nullification of land grants.

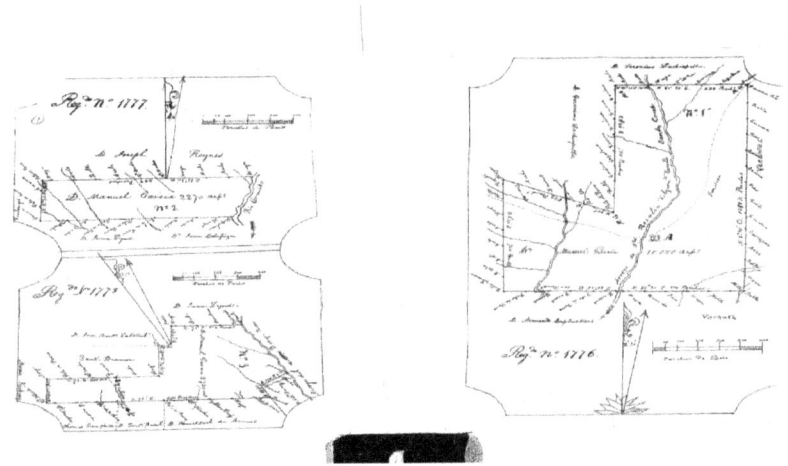

Garcia's land claim in East Feliciana Parish from the Vicente Sebastián Pintado collection.

Fast forward to 1836, Manuel Garcia faced a hurdle in his land ownership journey. Public records show that he filed a petition in the United States District Court for the Eastern District of Louisiana. The petition addressed a concerning situation. Samuel Lee, a resident of Louisiana, had either encroached upon Garcia's land or claimed ownership of a portion, if not the entirety, of Garcia's land. This cloud of uncertainty cast a shadow over Garcia's land ownership, raising doubts and concerns about the future of his property. Naturally, he took legal actions.

Following the legal proceedings, Manuel Garcia made the decision to sue Samuel Lee regarding a 10,000-arpent parcel of land situated in Louisiana. Garcia alleged that Lee had unlawfully occupied the land and refused to relinquish it. Seeking justice, Garcia filed a lawsuit in which he requested the court to order Lee to return the land and compensate him with $10,000 in damages.

Lee received a summons to appear before the district court in New Orleans on the third Monday of May in 1836. It was made clear that if Lee failed to appear in court, the ruling would be made against him in absentia. Therefore, the lawsuit between Manuel Garcia and Samuel Lee commenced on January 26th, 1836, in the Louisiana District Court. Garcia put forth his claim, asserting that he had purchased 15,000 arpents of land in Louisiana from the Spanish government on September 1st, 1806. To support his case, Garcia presented a deed of sale, along with plots and surveys as evidence.

On May 17th, 1836, Samuel Lee, as a resident of Feliciana Parish, Louisiana, challenged the lawsuit. Lee vehemently denied all of Garcia's assertions, including the authority of the Spanish government to sell the land and their control over the territory at that time. Essentially, Lee argued that the court lacked jurisdiction in the matter.

After a postponement on June 1st, 1836, requested by Garcia's attorney, the case finally went to trial on December 28th, 1836. However, the trial did not conclude on that day. The court decided to continue the case, granting Lee's attorney more time to raise objections after receiving documents from Garcia.

On February 27th, 1837, the Louisiana District Court rendered its verdict in the lawsuit between Manuel Garcia and Samuel Lee. Following months of legal proceedings, the court ruled in favor of Samuel Lee, the defendant. As a result, Manuel Garcia's lawsuit contesting Lee's possession of the land was dismissed. Additionally, the court ordered Garcia to cover the court costs associated with the case.

After the court ruling in favor of Samuel Lee, Garcia remained undeterred and determined to fight for what he believed was rightfully his. On March 3rd, 1837, both parties agreed to include specific documents from the case in the official record to be sent to the Supreme Court of the United States. This indicated that Manuel Garcia decided to appeal the district court's decision, hoping for a favorable reversal.

The legal battle continued, with the details of the initial court case remaining somewhat mysterious. However, it is clear that Garcia was dissatisfied with the outcome. Driven by his determination to secure his land, he took his fight to the highest court in the land. On March 13th, 1837, Garcia appealed the lower court's decision to the Supreme Court of the United States. The ultimate ruling by the Supreme Court went against Garcia. Manuel Garcia's unwavering resolve to pursue justice and reclaim his land propelled his heirs to seek further legal recourse. (Peters 1838)

Following years of appeals to Congress and the courts by family including Manuel J Garcia, his son, a subsequent ruling by the Supreme Court on January 22, 1887, granted the heirs of Manuel Garcia y Muniz the option to purchase 163.31 acres of public lands for one dollar twenty-five cents per acre. (Government Printing Office 1896)

Captain Manuel Garcia not only found himself embroiled in a tense legal battle once but twice. In 1804, he found himself in court against D.B. Morgan, an American surveyor. The situation stemmed from a prior incident where Spanish authorities, including Garcia, had arrested Morgan on Spanish soil. However, Morgan wasn't one to be easily detained. He managed to escape while aboard a Spanish galley captained by Garcia and make his way to New Orleans.

Upon arrival, a furious Morgan sought legal recourse. He filed a lawsuit against Garcia, demanding a significant sum of money - upwards of six hundred dollars as compensation for his arrest and the confiscation of his property. The legal system lurched into action. Sheriff Louis Kerr, acting on a court order, attempted to apprehend Captain Garcia. Garcia, however, refused to comply. He stood his ground, citing orders from his superiors and declaring he would only yield to force.

The situation grew more complicated when Governor Folch, then residing in New Orleans, intervened. Though indisposed, the Governor's son delivered a message - Garcia was instructed to resist arrest and not provide bail. This legal matter was fueled by the heated emotions surrounding the young Folch's "intemperate language" during his delivery of the orders.

The situation surrounding Captain Garcia's arrest escalated dramatically. As the room where the standoff occurred filled with people, the tension grew thick. Many of them were armed Spaniards. However, Sheriff Kerr tried to maintain control and hesitated on bringing in reinforcements initially. He opted to delay the arrest for a few minutes, hoping for intervention from Governor Claiborne, the

Marquis of Casa Calvo, and Governor Folch. He believed that some communication between the two could defuse the situation. Garcia's defense hinged on the argument that Governor Claiborne's authorization for Spanish officers to travel through the ceded territory offered him protection under international law and the good faith of the American government. Leaving Garcia with his supporters, Sheriff Kerr conferred with Judge Prevost. The Judge's response was unequivocal: the writ must be enforced, and the Sheriff faced the consequences of failing to do so. (Gayarre 1866)

Back at Garcia's residence, the Sheriff, aware of the growing crowd – estimated at over two hundred restless individuals – bolstered his forces with a corporal and three additional men from the guardhouse. However, upon arrival, the situation turned hostile. Swords were drawn by Garcia's associates, and the Sheriff's limited manpower proved insufficient to apprehend him.

Finally, a detachment of U.S. troops under Lieutenant Wilson's command arrived. Faced with this superior force, Garcia's defiance waned. He surrendered, bringing a temporary end to the tense standoff. Sheriff Kerr's report to Governor Claiborne on November 17th, 1804, documented the dramatic turn of events.

This episode laid bare the underlying political complexities of the era. A seemingly straightforward legal matter transformed into a potential catalyst for a larger conflict. The show of force by Garcia's supporters and the intervention of the U.S. military underscored the fragile peace in the region.

The news of Garcia's arrest sent shockwaves through Spanish authorities. The Marquis of Casa Calvo was brimming with indignation. He penned a fiery letter to Governor Claiborne and vehemently argued that Garcia had acted solely under the orders of his superiors in Spanish territory. Therefore, he could not be held accountable on American soil.

Claiborne bristled at the accusatory tone directed towards him. His response, delivered on November 16th, was equally defiant. He curtly acknowledged Casa Calvo's letter and made it explicitly clear that Captain Garcia's arrest stemmed from a legitimate legal process initiated by the Superior Court of the territory.

Claiborne further asserted that the judiciary operated independently, free from his influence. He emphasized that if the arrest was indeed deemed unlawful, the court would undoubtedly release Garcia upon a proper application. Claiborne expressed his bewilderment at the outrage displayed by Casa Calvo and Governor Folch, finding their behavior completely unwarranted. He took particular offense to specific verbal messages relayed by Casa Calvo, deeming them not only "derogatory to the Government" he represented but also "personally offensive" to himself. He further acknowledged learning of equally "exceptionable language" used by Governor Folch. Claiborne left no room for misinterpretation – such threats would have no bearing on his commitment to his duty. A prolonged exchange of letters ensued between Casa Calvo and Claiborne.

The situation finally reached a resolution. As per Claiborne's communication on November 22nd, both parties agreed to let the judiciary handle the matter. Claiborne expressed satisfaction that Casa Calvo finally acknowledged the only appropriate path - allowing the legal system to determine Garcia's fate. Whether Claiborne's prior authorization for Governor Folch's passage through the territory granted Garcia immunity from arrest remained a question for the court to decide. However, Claiborne expressed confidence that the court would deliver a just verdict.

Claiborne was never allowed to enjoy long any degree of undisturbed tranquility. His tenure was a continuous exercise in navigating diplomatic tightropes. No sooner had he settled the Garcia controversy, another conflict arose with Casa Calvo. This time, the friction stemmed from his refusal to enforce judgments rendered by Spanish authorities against certain individuals. Casa Calvo vehemently protested this decision, arguing that Claiborne's stance crippled his ability to collect outstanding debts owed to the Spanish crown.

Claiborne, however, stood firm. In a final note to the Marquis, he explained the limitations imposed by American law. He clarified that only judgments issued by U.S. courts could be directly enforced. Judgments from foreign courts, regardless of their standing, were considered mere evidence and required validation by an American court before any action could be taken. Claiborne emphasized that the territorial courts were accessible to Casa Calvo, offering him a legitimate avenue to address any grievances.

Another thorny issue that plagued Claiborne's administration was the entrenched practice of slave trade. The newly established American regime aimed to abolish this trade, although these practices were quite prevalent during Spanish rule. Enforcing this new policy proved challenging. Claiborne faced the near-impossible task of completely shutting down the smuggling of slaves. Spanish territories neighboring the Louisiana Purchase served as a convenient conduit for this illegal activity. Slaves were smuggled through a network of lakes, bayous, and waterways, finding their way into districts like East Baton Rouge and Feliciana.

Accusations of turning a blind eye to the trade swirled around Claiborne. In a letter to the President on November 25th, he vehemently defended his stance. He reiterated his personal abhorrence for the slave trade and expressed his sincere desire to see an end to this barbaric practice.

However, Claiborne found himself caught in a difficult situation. The local populace was accustomed to relying on slave labor, so they were naturally opposed to any restrictions on the trade. Even prominent figures openly expressed their agitation at any suggestion of restricting the trade. This made it nearly impossible for Claiborne to unilaterally enforce the new policy without prior legal authorization or explicit instructions from the federal government. (De Bow's Review 1866)

Documents have revealed that Manuel Garcia actively participated in this commerce as well, buying and selling enslaved individuals. A 32-year-old enslaved individual from Guinea was sold to Etienne Lepine for 330 piastres; Antoine Peytavin of St. John Parish acquired a slave from Garcia in exchange for 340 pounds of indigo, and Jacques Masicot facilitated the sale of another enslaved person owned by Garcia to Nicolas Demanche for 330 piastres. An intriguing record details a situation where Nicolas Demanche expressed dissatisfaction with the health of a slave purchased from Garcia through Masicot. Consequently, Demanche returned the enslaved individual and received a partial reimbursement for the time they were in his possession. (Gandolfo 2014)

For Manuel Garcia, the year 1804 wasn't just defined by legal battles. In April of that year, he assumed command of the schooner "Favorita" and other coast guard vessels. He was entrusted with safeguarding the Spanish interests along the Florida coastline between Pensacola and St. Marks. This appointment placed him directly on the frontlines, protecting Spanish territories from potential threats.

A year later in April 1805, Garcia's courage and resourcefulness were tested again. He found himself engaged in a close-quarter fight with an armed British vessel. His bravery shone through as he emerged victorious, not only capturing the enemy crew and officers but also securing a significant portion of their artillery.

Furthermore, in May 1805, he was entrusted with another critical mission – captaining the schooner "Proseopina" on a voyage to Vera Cruz, Mexico. His objective was to secure much-needed funds for West Florida. The journey was fraught with danger, as Garcia encountered enemy ships along the way. However, his determination and exceptional skills got him through. He successfully delivered a substantial sum of 150,000 Mexican dollars back to Pensacola, proving his mettle as a dependable leader.

The years between 1807 and 1810 saw Garcia actively involved in transporting vital supplies, reinforcements, and even monetary resources for West Florida. An intriguing instance stands out from 1808. Commanding three ships operating near New Orleans, he managed to successfully smuggle supplies from Louisiana to Pensacola, defying the Embargo Act imposed by the United States.

As the flames of the Mexican War of Independence erupted in 1810, Garcia's loyalty to the Spanish crown became increasingly undeniable. Stationed at Vera Cruz, he actively participated in the royalist cause. Several expeditions were undertaken under his command, aimed at transporting troops and supplies to quell the rebellion.

Garcia's heroism extended beyond wartime logistics. In 1812, the richly laden brigantine "Black" met with disaster, running aground near Vera Cruz. Despite facing a formidable challenge – insurgents positioned both on land and at sea – Garcia led a daring rescue operation. His courage and strategic thinking secured the rescue of the crew, passengers, and a significant portion of the ship's cargo. Similar acts of bravery were displayed in 1812 and 1813, where his interventions proved instrumental in ensuring the safe passage of critical supplies and personnel for the royalist forces.

In 1813, Garcia found himself confronted with a dire situation in Vera Cruz - a city lacking essential supplies and funds. However, his resourcefulness shone through once again. He sailed to New Orleans in his schooner and secured provisions, undertaking this mission without any financial gain for himself.

Beyond his military and commercial pursuits, Garcia's talents extended to geographical exploration. In late 1815 and early 1816, he charted the Rio Grande and surrounding coast. Garcia's detailed maps and strategic plans provided the Captain-General with invaluable knowledge of the region, and potentially influenced military decisions and future exploration.

Manuel Garcia's life remained tethered to political and military events even after the Mexican War of Independence subsided. A significant event during this period was the arrival of Francisco Javier Mina in 1816. Mina was a celebrated Spanish guerrilla fighter who had his sights set on liberating Mexico from Spanish rule. Garcia remained loyal to the Spanish crown and actively opposed Mina's efforts. Historical records show him commanding the frigate "Sabina" in an expedition against Mina's forces in May 1817. His actions were recognized, and he was awarded a shield of distinction. (J. D. Holmes, Dramatis Peronae 1965)

Garcia's expertise wasn't confined to military campaigns. His skills as a naval commander shone brightly in 1818. Patrolling the coast of Campeche, he successfully captured a schooner and a polacre, along with their cargo. Days later, he displayed courage by intercepting a pirate vessel and rescuing captured schooners. Moreover, Manuel Garcia sent fifteen boxes of sugar to Charleston from Havana, evidently praising the Editor of the Charleston Courier for publishing a letter supporting his ongoing operations against pirates.

In 1819, he received intelligence about the activities of Mariano Renovales, a former Spanish general suspected of plotting against both the United States and Mexico. Garcia's investigation revealed Renovales' plan to misuse funds from the Royal Treasury. Taking decisive action, Garcia was able to prevent this scheme and later apprehended Renovales upon his departure from New Orleans. Garcia's dedication to the Spanish crown was acknowledged through various awards and appointments. In 1825, he was designated a member of the Permanent Military Executive Commission by the Captain-General of Cuba.

In 1829, he was entrusted with the mission of transporting over 500 Spanish troops who had departed Mexico following the war. These soldiers, under the command of Brigadier Isidro Barradas, marked the final remnants of Spanish military presence on Mexican soil. Garcia's role involved not only securing the necessary transport ships but also provisioning these troops. He sailed from Havana under the command of the Royal Navy's Captain-General, and upon reaching Tampico, ensured the soldiers received much-needed rice rations.

Back in Havana by March 1830, Garcia resumed his duties as a judge on the military commission. His loyalty and dedication were further acknowledged later that year when he was appointed commander of the Havana Deposit for Transient Military Officers. Financial contributions also highlighted his commitment. Records show him donating over $1800 to the war effort throughout his service, with an additional voluntary contribution in 1809.

Military honors were also bestowed upon Garcia in recognition of his service. In 1812, he was promoted to Lieutenant in the Royal Armies, followed by a brevet Colonelcy in 1826. His dedication continued, and in 1831, he was appointed Second-in-Command of the Cuban Infantry.

Manuel Garcia's life wasn't without its share of personal tragedies. In 1827, a suspicious fire destroyed a large house he owned in Pensacola, Florida. Despite this setback, his career continued to flourish. Just a few months later, he was appointed commander of the Deposit of Transient Military Officers in Havana, solidifying his position within the Spanish military structure. Moreover, in the same year, he received the prestigious Royal Cross of the Military Order of San Hermenegildo.

In the 1830s, Cuba seemed to have become Manuel's new home. After years of service, he was finally stationed there, likely feeling a sense of stability. He even rose through the ranks, becoming Second-in-Command of the Cuban Infantry in 1831. (J. D. Holmes, Dramatis Peronae 1965)

Then, in 1845, everything changed. News trickled in from New Orleans, spreading like wildfire. Manuel Garcia, now a Colonel, had been assassinated in Havana. A soldier named Juan Bataroni was responsible. However, justice was served swiftly; Bataroni was executed and paid the ultimate price for his crime. (Daily Atlas 1845)

Manuel's final resting place is next to his wife, who quickly followed him to the grave, in St. Charles Borromeo Church, back in Louisiana. In New Orleans, banks printed a $10.00 dollar bill, in French, called a "dix." The Americans familiar with the French note used to say as they passed the "Red Church", "we are now in the 'dixie' land." Hence, the "Red Church" marked the entrance and innovation of the term Dixieland. (Gandolfo)

The last chapter of Manuel Garcia's life was bleak, but his whole existence was characterized by more than just military actions and battles. He was a devoted soldier who was promoted to the highest ranks and a family man who made significant contributions to the prominent circles of Louisiana and West Florida. Colonel Garcia's tale is more than just one of war; it represents a broader, multi-faceted life that ended too soon. There he left behind a legacy of commitment and service that will forever be remembered in the tranquil grounds of the Old Red Church.

∽◯

Chapter Three:
The Rise Of Felix Garcia

Felix Jean de Dios Garcia, a man whose very name whispered of his rich heritage, entered the world in 1803 amidst the vibrant city of New Orleans. At the time, New Orleans itself was a city of contrasts. Bustling commerce thrived alongside severe poverty. However, his arrival marked a new chapter in a family already deeply entrenched in Louisiana's history. The Garcia name resonated alongside prominent families like the Massicots and Arnaults, ensuring young Felix a life steeped in tradition and opportunity.

Felix's parents, Manuel Garcia and Aimée Massicot, recognized the importance of education in shaping their son's future. They provided him with the finest instruction available, enrolling him in prestigious schools that nurtured his intellect and potential. As Felix matured, they made the decision to send him to a military academy in Pensacola. The regimented environment instilled discipline in him and prepared him for the challenges and responsibilities that lay ahead. Military school proved to be a breeding ground for Felix's talents. He flourished in his studies, excelling academically. The academy instilled in him a sense of order and perseverance, qualities that would serve him well in the years to follow. Felix's brother, Carlos, also attended school in Pensacola, studying law.

However, life beyond the academic walls presented a different reality. Felix had risen to the esteemed position of Grand Master of the Louisiana Masons. This prestigious role spoke volumes about his character. He was a man who, like the Freemasons themselves, valued reason and enlightenment over blind faith and bigotry.

It is known that Felix was a gentleman with a decidedly French air, his gaze seemingly fixed a century into the future. He possessed an undeniable fastidiousness, evident in the way one hand rested neatly on his waistcoat, its fingers long and beautifully shaped. The prominent index finger, tapering towards the light, spoke of an artistic soul, and a plain band adorned his middle finger. Perhaps he was a musician who once coaxed sweet melodies from a spinet with those very hands. One glance at his hands revealed a life untouched by manual labor. His profession, then, remained a tantalizing mystery. Perhaps, some dared to speculate, he was a shrewd and seasoned politician, his intelligence accentuated by a prominent, "heavenly nose," a telltale sign of a keen intellect. Another venture he made was that he might be a highly skilled surgeon of his day.

Felix Garcia was undeniably a man of many contradictions. He was a Mason of high degree, yet his hands held the grace of an artist. He possessed a sharp mind, yet a hint of romanticism lingered in his features. His upbringing, too, reflected these contradictions. While his father, Manuel, was stationed at a military post in Pensacola during Felix's boyhood, the roots of his upbringing lay in the widow

Massicot's plantation on the Mississippi River. This was where Felix spent his formative years, amidst the sprawling landscapes and complex dynamics of plantation life. (Garcia 1954)

It was here that Felix encountered stories that would shape his worldview. One such tale was that of Slave Lubin. However, another gruesome discovery unfolded in St. Charles Parish in early fall of 1807. A local magistrate, Pierre Saint Amand, stumbled upon the body of a white man while inspecting a boat along the coast. The victim bore clear signs of foul play – three brutal wounds to the head. The body was buried by Saint Amand's slaves near the plantation of Widow Massicot. Later that same day, Saint Amand received word of a noisy gathering of slaves at the Widow's estate. Upon investigation, suspicious items – meat and tafia – were found in the slave driver Lubin's cabin. This discovery, coupled with the fact that Saint Amand had seen his merchant brother, Baptiste, wearing similar clothing to the deceased just two days prior, sparked a suspicion of cruelty and wrongdoing. (St. Charles Parish 1807)

With a growing conviction that Lubin was the perpetrator, Pierre Saint Amand, fueled by a thirst for justice, enlisted his brother Silvain and together they descended upon Widow Massicot's plantation. Arriving with a sense of urgency, they sought out Charles and Augustin, the Widow's sons. Wasting no time, Pierre revealed his plan to apprehend Lubin, the slave driver. To bolster his case, he laid out the incriminating evidence – the suspicious bounty of meat and tafia discovered in Lubin's cabin. These items bore an uncanny resemblance to the very wares a recently deceased peddler had been known to carry. As if this weren't enough, Pierre added another unsettling detail – a personal encounter with his own brother, Baptiste, just two days prior on September 18, 1807.

Baptiste, he disclosed, had been sporting clothing eerily similar to that of the murdered man. Charles and Augustin, taken aback by this cascade of revelations, readily confirmed the presence of the suspicious provisions in Lubin's quarters. Their shock quickly turned to a grim acceptance, and they offered no resistance to the apprehension of their mother's slave. Capitalizing on their cooperation, Saint Amand swiftly took Lubin into custody. He then proceeded to Widow Massicot's residence to retrieve the stolen goods. With both the captured suspect and the recovered evidence in tow, Saint Amand marched towards Judge Saint Martin's house, determined to see justice served.

In a bid to solidify his case, Pierre Saint Amand presented further details from his investigation into the peddler's murder. He revealed testimonies from Bastien and Scipion, two slaves belonging to Widow Massicot's estate. These slaves claimed to have assisted Lubin, the plantation's foreman, in carrying merchandise like cured meat, hardtack, and fishing lines to his cabin. As compensation for their help, they were given a small amount of tafia, a potent rum. Bastien further recounted encountering a white peddler near the river on September 18th, who refused to trade with him.

Additional inconsistencies arose during questioning of Lubin by Augustin Massicot, along with slaves Félix, François Créole, Bastien, and Scipion. This prompted the summoning of Judge Pierre Bauchet Saint Martin to the plantation to interview François Sannom, another slave who was unfortunately too weak to provide a sworn statement earlier.

Arriving on September 28th, 1807, Judge Saint Martin obtained a statement from a standing François Sannom. Sannom described seeing the peddler on September 18th, noting that he was an older man of average build, dressed in a white shirt and handkerchief. According to Sannom, other slaves relayed that the peddler had given Lubin a chicken to cook and had been selling cured meat. These testimonies further implicated Lubin in the peddler's demise, leading to his continued detention and the request for a military officer for protection.

As the investigation into the peddler's murder deepened, Pierre Saint Amand and the court delved into additional testimonies and scrutinized evidence. Lubin, the foreman of Widow Massicot's plantation, was brought back for further questioning. Despite his claims of innocence, inconsistencies in his story compared to others raised red flags. A shroud discovered in Lubin's possession, believed to belong to the deceased peddler, was unconvincingly explained by Lubin as a gift from two unknown Americans. Furthermore, syrup bottles found with Lubin were linked by the court to a peddler named Arnaud, who was presumed to be the victim. The accumulating evidence painted a damning picture: Lubin, with the help of slaves Bastien and Scipion, likely transported stolen goods from the murdered peddler to his cabin sometime between September 18th and 19th, 1807. To bolster their case, witnesses confirmed no knowledge of Lubin's supposed accomplice, "Louis du Cap." Based on the mounting evidence and conflicting statements, the judge and jury reached a unanimous verdict: Lubin was found guilty of both premeditated murder and theft.

Based on the evidence presented, including witness statements and circumstantial proof, Lubin was found guilty and sentenced to death under the brutal Dark Code. This code, unlike the Black Code, mandated the execution of enslaved people for crimes against white individuals. The court appointed Pierre Bauchet Saint Martin, a civil and criminal judge, and another person to oversee Lubin's execution. They were also tasked with informing the parish priest so he could offer religious consolation to Lubin before his death. This was done with the guidance and assent of Charles Perret and Francois Brou, the proprietors of property nearby.

Perhaps the most significant event during Felix's boyhood was the slave revolt of 1811. The rebellion unfolded directly across the Mississippi River from where Felix may have spent a portion of his childhood on Widow Massicot's plantation. The region witnessed the largest organized slave rebellion in American history. Fueled by the successful Haitian Revolution, over two hundred enslaved people, led by Charles Deslondes, embarked on a daring march downriver. For two days, they carried flags, banners, and drums, determined to achieve freedom. However, their aspirations were met with a harsh reality. Surprised by a detachment of troops, the rebels were forced to retreat. They subsequently encountered a local militia, effectively quelling their attempt at liberation.

The aftermath of the revolt proved tragic. Approximately twenty enslaved people lost their lives in the clashes, while casualties were also sustained among the white population. Several buildings along the route were consumed by flames. Following a swift tribunal at Destrehan Plantation, forty-five individuals were sentenced to death and summarily executed by firing squad on their original plantations. In a grotesque act of intimidation, their heads were severed and displayed on poles as a warning against future uprisings. (Yoes III 2005)

News of the rebellion reverberated throughout the nation, dominating headlines in newspapers across the country. This event served as a catalyst for the enactment of even more restrictive slave codes, not only in Louisiana but throughout the South. Both enslaved and free blacks faced a harsher reality as a direct consequence of this audacious act of defiance.

Felix's upbringing might have instilled a sense of distrust between him and the enslaved people around him. Historical records show that on April 30th, 1840, Felix purchased a number of enslaved people from the Whitney Plantation. However, whispers followed these transactions, painting a troubling picture of Felix's conduct as a slave owner. Allegedly, the treatment he dished out was far from kind, ultimately leading the enslaved people he bought to take a desperate step. According to Felix, they attempted to poison him by lacing grinding glass and putting it in his berries which they fed to him as a dessert. Fortunately for them, the legal system found them not guilty. Importantly, Louisiana had a legal code, "The Code Noir," established in 1724, which outlined some basic rights for enslaved people. This code mandated that they be instructed in Catholicism, receive allotments of food and clothing, and enjoy Sundays off. Additionally, it offered them the right to petition a public prosecutor if they felt mistreated. (Rogers 2020)

Amidst the dark political climate, Felix's life took a significant turn in 1826. He embarked on a new chapter in his life, marrying Marie Francoise Massicot in a ceremony likely held at St. Charles Borromeo Catholic Church in Louisiana. Marie Francoise was actually Felix's first cousin, cementing their union within the familial bonds of their community. However, the details of their wedding are shrouded in mystery due to the unfortunate loss of records in a fire, leaving behind only fragmented memories and anecdotes passed down through generations.

Marie Francoise, born to Jean-Baptiste Massicot and Eulalie Daspit St. Amand on December 11, 1806, brought with her a lineage deeply rooted in the Louisiana soil. Her connection to Felix not only tied their families closer but also intertwined their destinies in ways unforeseen. (Gandolfo 2014)

Together, Felix and Marie Francoise embarked on a journey of marriage and family, blessed with children who would carry their legacy forward. Among their offspring were Charles Manuel Garcia, Estelle

Elizabeth Garcia, Felix Eugene Garcia, Manuel Etienne Garcia, and Marie Aimée Garcia. However, out of all their children, only Marie Aimée Garcia survived to grow into adulthood. (Zeringue 1828-1840)

Tragically, Felix and Marie's blissful union was cut short as well by the untimely passing of Marie Francoise in 1835. Left behind with one surviving daughter, Marie Aimée Garcia, Felix faced the daunting task of navigating life's challenges as a widower. However, there was a silver lining. Through Marie Francoise's Massicot lineage, Marie Aimée inherited a significant amount of property and even slaves.

Felix wouldn't remain a widower for long. In 1836, he married Matilde Arnault, daughter of Jean Eleanor Arnault. This union held a particular significance as well. It was from Jean Arnault that Felix had earlier acquired his first plot of land. Unlike his previous marriage, this union with Louise Mathilde remained childless.

Felix's ambition extended beyond the walls of his home. By 1831, he had set his sights on acquiring land, and he purchased a plot near present-day Wallace, Louisiana. This strategic acquisition placed his property right at the parish boundary between St. Charles and St. John Parish on the St. John side, the right bank of the Mississippi. The land marked a significant step towards establishing himself. Historical records suggest the purchase originated with Jean Arnault, adding another layer to Felix's network of business dealings. The wedding was attended by Francois Trépagnier, Patrice Arroyo, Hyppolite Trépagnier, Faustin Fortier, Aimée Massicot, and Jean Eleanor Arnauld. (Wedding Certificate 1836)

This land deal wasn't his only foray into property acquisition. Just a year later, in 1832, Felix secured a loan from Citizens Bank, likely to further expand his holdings. These early investments in land hinted at Felix's entrepreneurial spirit. Subsequently, Felix's life continued on an upward path, marked by both political ambition and a thirst for accumulation. By 1836, his reputation and influence had grown considerably, culminating in his election as a State Senator from St. John Parish. This political achievement solidified his status as a prominent figure within the community.

However, his focus wasn't solely on politics. He also took part in business ventures. In 1842, he expanded his holdings yet again, acquiring property within the bustling city of New Orleans itself. This move showed his desire to diversify his assets beyond solely agricultural pursuits.

In June 1842, Felix Garcia acquired eleven lots of ground in the city of New Orleans from the probate court in favor of his daughter Aimée Marie Garcia after the passing of Marie Francoise Massicot, Felix's first wife. The eleven lots were roughly bounded by Esplanade, Robertson, and Villere Streets. Felix mortgaged the lots for $7,030.50. (Blanc 1842)

Upon reorganization of the State Senate after the election of 1842, Felix was elected President of that body, even though the Democrats had a majority. He received a unanimous vote. Felix was described as an "adamant whig." Felix was first elected to the State Senate in 1836. (The Daily Picayune 1844)

Back in St. John Parish, Felix continued to invest in land and enslaved people. Some of these acquisitions involved partnerships, such as the venture with Achille Loreo on one particular plot. The year 1846 proved particularly fruitful for him. Felix, along with Adolphe Sorapuru, struck a significant deal, acquiring a vast tract of land with prime river frontage at Bonnet Carre Point. Recognizing the fertile potential of the land at Bonnet Carre Point, modern-day Lucy, Felix likely saw an opportunity to cultivate sugarcane, a crop in high demand and well-suited to the Louisiana climate. In 1844 Garcia & Sorapuru produced 1,015 hogsheads of sugar. (Yoes III 2005)

Adolphe Sorapuru was an outlier in Louisiana Culture. His common-law wife Andora LeBlanc was mulatto, albeit they could not be legally married in Louisiana culture at the time. They were married by Judge Leblanc who fathered Andora with Josephine Foucher who was a woman of color. The wedding was not recorded. Adolphe was the Recorder of Mortgages in St. John Parish. He and Adorea owned a small plantation and did so without acquiring slaves. They hired free blacks and paid them workers' wages while treating them as employees. (Sorapuru 1870)

"Sorapuru House." *Mon Cher*, June 20: 12. Photo from Louisiana Studies in Historic Preservation.

http://www.laheritage.org/CreoleHeritage/Color.html

Constructed in 1825 by St John the Baptist Parish's first judge, Joseph Terence (LeBlanc) de Villeneuve, as his home in Lucy. It also served as the first parish courthouse until 1847 when the parish seat was moved down the road to Edgard. It is listed on the National Register of Historic Places. It is one of the last remaining homes built of the French Creole architecture. Felix would have had a similar home nearby. (Darensbourg, Marlene. 2003)

Felix's influence extended beyond land purchases and partnerships. He was a member of the board of directors at Citizens Bank. This position likely played a role in another key development in 1846. Matilde, Felix's second wife, was due to inherit property and slaves from her father, Jean Arnault. However, a closer inspection revealed that the debts associated with this inheritance outweighed the value of the assets themselves. Through negotiations with Citizens Bank, Felix was able to secure both the land and the slaves for himself and his wife.

Felix's political astuteness wasn't just confined to his role as a State Senator. In the winter of 1845, Louisiana embarked on a crucial endeavor - the drafting of a new state constitution. The existing document, crafted in 1812, no longer reflected the realities of a rapidly changing state. There were plentiful criticisms of the old constitution – it was seen as archaic, undemocratic, and resistant to modernization. In this pivotal moment, Felix rose to a position of significant authority. He was elected president of the convention tasked with crafting the new constitution. This role placed him at the center of a momentous debate that would shape the future of Louisiana.

One specific issue that ignited Felix's passion was the practice of dueling. Newspapers of the time, such as the Jeffersonian Republic, documented Felix's stance on this contentious topic. While his religious beliefs made him personally opposed to dueling and the concept of settling disputes through violence, he took a nuanced approach. He believed that the proposed penalties for dueling were insufficient to truly eradicate the practice. Interestingly, he argued that other societal ills, such as gambling, were even more destructive. He highlighted the devastating impact of gambling – not just the loss of life, but also the shame and misery inflicted on families left behind. (Ghent University 1858)

Felix's address on dueling reflects both his moral convictions and his pragmatic understanding of the challenges facing Louisiana. He sought solutions that addressed the root causes of violence rather than simply punishing the act itself. This glimpse into his thought process reveals a man grappling with complex social issues and seeking to shape a better future for his state. Some thought his oration was peculiar as a family letter says Felix fought in a duel, but we cannot verify it. (Garcia 1954)

In 1845, during the Louisiana Constitutional Convention, Felix Garcia found himself at the center of a heated debate – dueling. One side, championed by Koulmy, condemned dueling as a barbaric remnant, destined to be discarded alongside the societal ills that birthed it. This faction believed cooperation and mutual respect were the cornerstones of a more civilized future. The proposed Louisiana constitution reflected this stance, potentially stripping political rights from those who participated in duels. Marigny, another convention member, rose in passionate defense of the practice. He argued that society wouldn't tolerate serious offenses without a means for the aggrieved to seek satisfaction.

Felix Garcia then entered the fray. Described as a visionary defending a seemingly lost cause, he rose with a voice that vibrated with intensity. He demanded a roll call, determined to expose those who hid behind the supposed impossibility of a challenge. This fiery response suggested a man who, while personally opposed to dueling based on his religion, possessed a deeper understanding of the social forces driving it. Perhaps he recognized that simply outlawing the practice wouldn't eradicate the underlying issues.

Years later, a controversy arose as a family letter surfaced, mentioning a duel involving Felix. Public records indicate his nephew, son of Manuel Garcia, the Sheriff of Jefferson Parish was involved in a duel. While no public record of a duel involving Felix himself existed, this family lore added another layer of complexity to his relationship with this debatable practice. It hinted that dueling might have touched Felix's life more personally than initially thought, perhaps leaving a lasting mark on him. (A Duel 1857)

While deeply involved in the momentous task of drafting a new Louisiana constitution, his personal life also saw a significant development in the winter of 1845. He met Magdalena Adrian, and their relationship resulted in the birth of a son, Charles Garcia, on November 24th, 1845. Little is known about Magdalena. She is said to be from Alsace. (O'Dell 1970)

Magdalena embarked on a journey to Le Havre, France. She returned with some of her family. Upon her return to Louisiana in May 1852, she fell ill with typhoid fever, necessitating three stays at Charity Hospital in New Orleans. After her arrival back from France, she found lodging with the Albert Manouvrier family near St. Mary's Assumption Church. Mr. Manouvrier, a talented musician, composed a martial tune and taught Magdalena's son, Charles, to play the violin. (Charity Hospital 1852)

Tragically, Magdalena passed away on January 3, 1853, and she was laid to rest in Lafayette Cemetery No. 1, located in the Garden District of what was then Jefferson, Louisiana.

Despite the controversies, there have been reports of Garcia's honorable acts as well. In a separate incident recounted in a newspaper clipping dated Thursday morning, September 23rd, 1847, aboard the steamboat F. M. Streck, a French passenger fell overboard upon the vessel's arrival at the Levee. Despite the bystanders' initial shock and suggestions on how to rescue the man, no action was taken. Some said, "Pitch him a rope;" another said, "Throw him out a pole;" but in the meantime the man sunk twice, and no one made an effort to seize him. Observing the perilous situation, Honorable Felix Garcia, also a passenger on the vessel, leaped into the river and grasped the drowning man, while his loyal negro servant bravely followed suit. The heroic efforts of Mr. Garcia and his servant resulted in the successful rescue, earning admiration from onlookers for their humanity and courage. (Daily Picayune 1847)

Moreover, Felix Garcia was held in high esteem for his public virtue and esteemed membership in the Freemasons of Louisiana. There's a notable incident that sheds light on his character; when he was invited to join a political movement by a distinguished individual, he declined. Instead, he chose to remain faithful to the principles of his Masonic order - a decision that garnered praise for his integrity and dedication.

Garcia's reputation extended far and wide, as evidenced by the attendance of numerous lodges at a tribute held in his honor. At this gathering, heartfelt expressions of admiration were shared which demonstrated Garcia's unwavering commitment to the values of Freemasonry. In recognition of his exemplary service, resolutions were drafted by committee members and unanimously approved. These resolutions expressed gratitude for Garcia's contributions to the Masonic order. They were scheduled to be presented at an upcoming meeting of the Grand Lodge of Louisiana, ensuring that Mr. Garcia's legacy would be duly acknowledged and celebrated by the broader Masonic community. Felix was President of the Etoile Polaire No. 1

Lodge and a member of numerous other lodges in New Orleans. (Democrat Advocate 1847)

Felix Garcia. Courtesy of the Grand Lodge of the State of Louisiana, Alexandria, LA.

"Is undeniably fastidious for one hand reposes neatly upon the lower waist coat in such a hand! It is soft and velvety paper in texture and long and beautifully shaped. The index finger is shown at full length and tapers into the light of the soul of an artist. Upon the middle finger, there is a plain hand ring frame that could speak to tell the tale of love, which was the kind of man whose hand sought many other hands. These core chips were perpetual, like the seasons had air. This photograph was taken and singled out by Amy Massicot, his future wife, who thought his love ship had come to anchor.

One thing that this man hand proclaims in no uncertain language is that he never did manual labor of any kind at any time in his life. His profession must need to be conjectural adventure guest one of my dared to guess in which little go on that outside of being a Mason high degree he might indeed be a too skillful somewhat cynical barrister at law is not less likely noted scientist of his day he is clearly intelligent with all his attribute romance heavenly nose is a big belonging only to keen t intellects whatever else such a beak might signify.

I like to fancy that his life pulse with music and poetry with such fine hands he must have had as an accomplishment on the side of the art of lightly sweeping stringed instruments to his songs are filing their sweet melodies on the spinet. If I were the proud possessor of two such perfect hands this gentleman of undoubtedly Castilian ancestry could boast, I would not have trusted one of them into a mere pocket there to lie unseen unsung, but it would have probably displayed them both the full and on this English advantage." (Garica, 1954)

In a letter dated November 5, 1847, from New Orleans, it was revealed that the State Commissioners, in collaboration with Lodge St. James, No. 47, at Baton Rouge, invited the Grand Lodge of Louisiana to preside over the ceremonial laying of the corner-stone for the new State House. Grand Master Felix Garcia, along with other officers and members of the Grand Lodge, attended the event on November 2nd, 1847. Amidst a gathering of approximately one hundred and fifty Masons, the ceremony was conducted with due reverence. Garcia, serving as the Grand Orator, delivered an eloquent speech in French, while another man was scheduled to give an address in English, though only brief remarks were made due to the lateness of the hour. (Grand Celebration 1847)

Felix Garcia influenced the political sphere in more ways than one. In the year 1848, the political landscape of Louisiana was abuzz with anticipation and excitement. With high hopes for P. Soulé's return to the U.S. Senate, Garcia witnessed a surprising twist in the state election results. Despite some initial setbacks caused by disunity among the Democrats, there was still a glimmer of hope for Louisiana's representation on the national stage. Remember at this time, the state legislature elected U.S. Senators.

As the Legislature came together amidst a cloud of uncertainty, the stage was set for a dramatic showdown as the Whigs had a majority in the legislature following the 1848 elections. John Slidell was the Democratic nominee for U.S. Senator, ready to bring honor to Louisiana with his distinguished service. On the opposing side stood D. F. Kenner - a Whig and character more familiar with the racetrack than the political arena.

The early ballots revealed a tied race, with Slidell holding a slight lead over Kenner. The results were made even more interesting by Kenner's surprising act of casting a vote for himself. It was an uncommon occurrence in senatorial elections.

Amidst all the intrigue and speculation, the current US Senator Pierre Soulé turned out to be a formidable contender as well. He captured the imagination of Louisianans with his powerful speeches and unwavering patriotism. His nomination on the third ballot reflected a triumph of principle over political maneuvering. (Singular But Glorious Result 1848)

Ultimately, the Whig party in the United States suffered a big loss. Even though they had more members in the Legislature, they ended up losing the election for a U.S. Senator and the State Printer to the Democrats. This happened because some Whig members either didn't show up or switched sides to vote for Democrats. One Whig member, Mr. Myles, who initially supported a Whig candidate, disappeared when it was time to vote. Some others changed their votes during the process, causing the defeat. Another member, Mr. Alexander Baldwin (Felix's soon to be ex-brother-in-law), also changed his vote, showing his loyalty only went so far. Felix Garcia was also among the members who strategically switched sides.

Felix defended his vote and criticism from the Bulletin in terms of severity upon the editor of that journal by stating that "he respected Slidell as a gentleman but had vast disagreements over politics." Pierre Soulé was a 32º Mason. Felix was elected Grand Master of the Louisiana Lodge and was also bestowed the 32º title. (Times Picayune 1848)

The year was 1848, a notable incident involved the defeat of Kenner and subsequent defeat for Slidell by Pierre Soulé. This series of events was marked by allegations of corruption and political maneuvering. Soulé, while preferred by some over Slidell due to perceived less prejudice from the Whigs, found himself embroiled in a bitter struggle against William S. Parham. Parham was motivated by zealous loyalty to the Whig party and sought to defeat Soulé, despite his innocence in the alleged Plaquemines fraud. The Whig press vilified Soulé and others, attributing treachery to those who opposed their interests.

The reflections of The New Orleans Bulletin on the defeat of the Whig party revealed the ever-changing tides of political fortune. Amidst the blame cast by the Whig party, Garcia was a major figure due to his role in shaping the electoral outcome. In conclusion, as we follow the tale of Felix Garcia's life, we see a man of ambition, contradiction, and a thirst for knowledge. Raised amidst Antebellum Louisiana and the harsh realities of slavery, he was a product of his time. He was a landowner and slave owner, a politician and a family man. He was a Mason who valued reason yet possessed a touch of the romantic. Through his journey, we see the complexities of life in the antebellum South, a society grappling with issues of race, class, and social change. Felix Garcia's legacy remains an enigma, a man of shadows and whispers, leaving us to wonder about the motivations that truly drove him.

Chapter Four:
Trials And Tribulations

The rhythmic clatter of iron wheels against steel tracks was a sound still unfamiliar to most American ears in the early 1830s. However, in the thriving port city of New Orleans, a new era of transportation was dawning. This revolution was primarily led by Felix Garcia - a man whose name would become synonymous with one of the South's earliest and most ambitious railroad ventures – the Mexican Gulf Railroad.

Despite coming from a modest background, Felix Garcia made a lasting impact on the Gulf region's transportation system. He was raised in the streets of Pensacola and New Orleans, far from the opulent plantation homes typical of the time. Rather, he lived in a little house at 310 Hospital Street, between Dauphine and Burgundy, and had no property to his name. His early years were a reflection of Bourbon Street's vibrant energy, where he probably took in the many ethnicities and trade that infused the city. Felix had modest origins, but his spirit of entrepreneurship took off from the start. He was instrumental in the founding of the Mexican Gulf Railroad in January 1836. With the advent of rail transportation, drayage methods such as ox-drawn carts quickly declined.

Before Felix Garcia steered the Mexican Gulf Railroad, the American South, particularly away from the major coastal cities, relied heavily on a network of waterways and slow, often treacherous, land routes. While canals offered some relief, they were limited in reach and often seasonally dependent. The arrival of railroads in the early 19th century revolutionized transportation. Unlike water-based routes confined by geography, railroads offered a more direct path, significantly reducing travel times for both passengers and goods. This efficiency promised economic growth. Farmers could transport crops to markets faster and at a lower cost, while manufactured goods could become more readily available throughout the region. The South, heavily reliant on agriculture, saw a particular boom as cotton and other key exports could be delivered to ports more efficiently. This rise of railroads not only transformed how goods moved, but also spurred the development of new towns and industries along established routes.

As Felix Garcia's vision for the Mexican Gulf Railroad continued to unfold, it extended its reach far beyond mere transportation. It became a conduit for exploration and cultural exchange along the Gulf Coast. One pivotal extension of the railroad network was the Shell Beach Railroad. The Shell Beach Railroad, an integral part of the Mexican Gulf Railroad's expansion, stretched from the streets of New Orleans to the serene shores of Shell Beach, formerly known as Proctorsville, located along the tranquil waters of Lake Borgne.

The Shell Beach Railroad station stood at the corner of Claiborne and Good Children streets. This was the starting point for a trip through beautiful St. Bernard Parish. Passengers would travel past sugar plantations, bustling towns, and unique communities that showed the mix of cultures along the Gulf Coast. One stop was Islingues, a settlement where people whose ancestors came from the Canary Islands kept their Spanish traditions alive. But the most interesting stop for many was St. Malo. Here, people with roots in the Philippines, mostly Malays, had created a new language by blending Tamil with Spanish. This reflected their heritage and the many influences that shaped their lives. Felix recognized the economic potential of connecting this popular spot to the city, and he seized the opportunity to be part of this endeavor.

Felix Garcia's involvement with the Mexican Gulf Railroad contributed to the development of transportation infrastructure in the region. In March 1837, the Mexican Gulf Railroad Company received its charter, amidst a period of speculative frenzy and wild improvement company planning. The company's capitalization stood at $1,000,000, which could be increased to $2,000,000 if needed. The stock was affordable, with shares priced at only $2 per 100 shares. Moreover, the company enjoyed tax exemptions for sixty years, reflecting the exuberance of the times. The legislature generously granted the seemingly favored railroad company three years to commence building the railroad and ten years to complete it.

The route chosen for the Mexican Gulf railroad seemed audacious, traversing swamps, shallow lakes, bayous, islands, and bays. However, Felix understood that the railroad's ultimate goal was to establish port facilities for New Orleans on the Gulf of Mexico, necessitating a crossing through the marshes to reach the sea. Undeterred by the challenges, Felix and his fellow visionaries began building the railroad even before the entire route was surveyed. It wasn't until 1839 - three years after the charter's passing, that a survey was conducted to assess the feasibility of the chosen path. The first forty-four miles, covering reasonably stable terrain, were feasible and passed through a level cultivated tract of land and a ridge of high timbered land belonging to the United States. However, the remaining twenty-eight miles posed quite a challenging obstacle. The route snaked through a firm marsh of no commercial value, teeming with wild fowl, fish, and oysters. It held a few precious shell banks, but the overall terrain was impractical. Felix and his companions faced the task of bridging this final stretch. (Reed 1966)

Despite the difficulties, Felix remained committed to his endeavor. His dedication to the Mexican Gulf Railroad, a position he held since the formation, allowed him to steer the company towards success. However, Felix's life was not without its challenges.

In May 1849, he found himself embroiled in a legal dispute with George Haltzman. The U.S. Circuit Court for the District of Louisiana ruled in favor of Haltzman, leading to a public sale of Felix's plantation situated on the right bank of the Mississippi River in St. Charles Parish. The sale included a steam engine that was a symbol of Felix's determination. (Le Courrier de la Louisiane 1849)

Felix Garcia's interests extended beyond the realm of railways. As a shrewd businessman and owner of eleven lots outside the French Quarter, he recognized the importance of drainage in combating the diseases that plagued New Orleans. Yellow fever and malaria, transmitted by mosquitoes, were endemic and periodically epidemic throughout the nineteenth century, causing high mortality rates among the city's residents. (History of New Orleans Drainage 1893)

During the administration of Mayor Louis Philippe de Roffignac from 1820 to 1828, a canal was dug in the rear of the American Quarter for drainage purposes. This canal, later known as the Melpomene Canal, aimed to alleviate the stagnant water that served as breeding grounds for disease-carrying mosquitoes. Another canal, the Poydras Canal, was dug through the middle of Faubourg Saint Marie, present-day Poydras Street. However, this canal fell into disuse due to neglect and became clogged with weeds and filth. The Marigny Canal, though unsatisfactory in its function, handled drainage below the city. It was clear that more comprehensive and effective drainage measures were needed to combat the mosquito-borne diseases that ravaged New Orleans.

During the 1830s and 1840s, New Orleans was ravaged by yellow fever and other diseases. Despite the devastating impact on the city's population, little was done by city officials to improve sanitary conditions. Sewage disposal methods remained unchanged since the French colonial period, with fecal matter being deposited in shallow, open pits or cesspools with porous bottoms. These pits would overflow during heavy rains and floods, leaving fecal matter in the yards and streets, creating a foul stench.

Occasionally, sanitary excavating companies would partially empty these pits, dumping the contents into the river beyond the city limits. However, even after these cleanings, the pits would emit a strong odor. Liquid household waste, including other filth, would end up in the gutters, which became clogged with excrement and other debris. In the hot summer months, the stagnant waters of the gutters would become covered with green slime. Ineffectual efforts were made to flush the gutters using sluices in the levees during river rises, but they were never entirely drained.

In 1835, a twenty-year charter was granted to the New Orleans Drainage Company, entrusting them with the crucial task of improving the city's drainage conditions. This marked a pivotal moment as the responsibility for drainage and sanitation shifted from individual residents and contractors to a city-administered public-private partnership. Felix Garcia found himself at the helm of this company, determined to tackle the pressing issues plaguing New Orleans.

The turning point came in 1840 when George T. Dunbar, the esteemed Engineer of the State of Louisiana, was commissioned to survey and conduct a topographical examination of the back section of the city. On February 17, 1840, Dunbar presented his findings to Felix Garcia, the president of the drainage company. This was a watershed moment as it marked the first drainage plan for the city that was based on New Orleans' topography and environmental conditions. It was also the first time that underground drainage was recommended for New Orleans.

Dunbar's report emphasized the urgent necessity for underground drains, stating that "no city in the Union needs underground drains more than New Orleans." His recommendations were intelligent and succinct, proposing the installation of two underground drains, five feet deep by four feet wide, under Canal Street, Bienville Street, St. Louis Street, and others, with meticulous consideration of their slopes. The visionary recommendations outlined in Dunbar's report were met with enthusiasm by the New Orleans Drainage Company. However, the city officials were not impressed by the report and did not act upon it. The aftermath of the panic of 1837 left the city with little resources for such a monumental project. The public opposed the plan due to the mortgages that would be placed on property to finance the undertaking, further complicating the situation.

Despite the setback, Felix Garcia and the drainage company remained committed to improving the city's sanitation. Their dedication to the cause was evident, but they were met with insurmountable challenges. The economic hardships of the time took their toll, and the drainage company eventually dissolved due to the challenging economic conditions.

Felix Garcia's ingenuity extended beyond his efforts in the realm of drainage and transportation. As a visionary entrepreneur, he sought to revolutionize the sugar industry, leveraging his creative mind to develop groundbreaking innovations.

In 1845, the Commissioner of Patents granted Felix Garcia a remarkable privilege – the exclusive right to manufacture and sell his self-invented machines for the production of sugar. This patent, valid for fourteen years, reflected the originality and value of his invention. The essence of Felix's innovation lay in his method of clarifying sugar juice. He discovered that by treating the saccharine liquid with an excess of lime and then with soap, the impurities could be effectively separated, leaving the liquid in a state of purity. The process, as detailed in the patent, involved first treating the liquid with an abundance of lime, which caused the impurities to be extracted from the solution. The subsequent addition of soap then reduced the lime and the impurities to a state where they could be easily removed, allowing the purified liquid to remain.

This ingenious technique revolutionized the sugar-making process, offering a more efficient and effective way to refine the precious commodity. Felix's patent granted him the exclusive right to manufacture, employ, and sell these machines, positioning him as a trailblazer in the industry. To ensure the protection of his invention, Felix was required to deposit a detailed model or plan of his machine with the secretary of state within one month of the patent's passage. This safeguard was put in place to prevent unauthorized individuals from replicating his design and undermining his exclusive privilege.

The impact of Felix's innovation was far-reaching. His patented machines for sugar manufacturing became a sought-after commodity, with the potential to transform the industry and improve the quality and efficiency of sugar production. As a former Louisiana sugar refiner, Felix Garcia attracted the interest of eminent scientists and scholars. Eventually, he was recognized by the Academy of Sciences in Paris.

When M. Basset presented the procedure to the Academy of Sciences, it was heralded as a revolutionary development in the field of sugar refinement. It was predicated on lime's well-known ability to react with fats to form alkaline soap. When a solution of soda and lime saccharate were combined, the soda stayed in solution in the liquid and the lime combined with the soap fat, setting the sugar free.

This method of sugar clarification was precise and delicate, requiring a careful flow of processes. Following an excess of lime clarification and impurity skimming, the liquid was chilled to a lower temperature than 104 degrees Fahrenheit. This was the exact moment when the soap solution was added and the mixture was gently swirled. After adding the soap to the mixture and carefully bringing it back to a boil, the temperature was suddenly dropped, which caused fresh scum to be removed.

As a result of this process, a calcareous soap was formed and all of the contaminants and extraneous materials in the liquid rose to the surface with it. Consequently, the Academy of Sciences in Paris recognized Garcia's method, demonstrating his great contribution to the science of sugar refinement.

The 1840s had been a period of prosperity for Felix Garcia, marked by groundbreaking innovations and entrepreneurial successes. However, the latter part of the decade proved to be a series of tumultuous challenges that tested his resilience and fortitude.

The devastating loss of the sugar house in St. John Parish, Louisiana, in March 1849 was a severe blow to Felix Garcia. The destruction of 100 hogsheads of sugar and molasses, estimated at a staggering $30,000, due to an uninsured fire, left him reeling from the financial and emotional toll. This tragic event was compounded by the foreclosure of the plantation originally purchased from Jean Eleanor Arnault, Felix's father-in-law, in May 1849. (New Orleans Bee 1849)

As if these setbacks were not enough, the year 1850 brought further tribulations. The first of many crevasse breaks was reported on the morning of the 29th of December, 1849, signaling the beginning of a series of natural disasters that would shake the foundations of Felix's endeavors. The disastrous crevasse at Bonnet Carré in the same year, with a break that spanned 7,000 feet, unleashed a torrent of water that inundated the entire parish on the left bank. The floodwaters were running with great force into Lake Pontchartrain, deluging the surrounding areas. (Times Picayune 1850)

Several planters, including Messrs. Oxley, Labranche, Finerews, Boulgay, Kamas, Armand, Felix Garcia, H. Phreys, and others, were affected by the flooding. In response, efforts were underway to construct levees and draining mechanisms to alleviate the pressure from the surplus water. Though it enabled the planters to prepare the ground for the next year's crop, the raging floodwaters destroyed crops, valuable property, and much of Felix's personal possessions, inflicting immeasurable losses.

The destructive force of the crevasse resulted in the destruction or washing away of twelve to fifteen dwellings. The impact of this disaster was not limited to planters alone, as numerous poor families and enslaved individuals also lost their homes. Approximately one hundred houses were deemed entirely uninhabitable. However, the impact on Felix Garcia's life was devastating as it flooded his sugar-houses.

Naturally, the partnership between Felix Garcia and his associate, Adolphe Sorapuru also faced insurmountable challenges in the aftermath of the devastating flood. The need to salvage what remained from the deluge, repair homes, and assist family members and neighbors in the wake of the destruction weighed heavily on their shoulders. The uncertainty of the plantation's future profitability, compounded by the significant losses incurred, led to the difficult decision to dissolve the partnership. (Sorapuru 1870)

In February of 1850, the Consolidated Association of Planters of Louisiana filed a suit seeking to foreclose on the mortgage, further exacerbating the already arduous situation. Despite the profound losses and the weight of the decisions made, Felix Garcia faced the aftermath with resilience and determination. The property was sold by judicial sale to Michael Thomassin Andry, marking the end of an era and the closure of a significant chapter in Felix's life.

In the midst of Felix Garcia's already burdened existence, fate dealt him another devastating blow. On a somber morning in New Orleans, the city awoke to the news of a tragic loss - the passing of Louise Mathilde Garcia, beloved wife of Felix Garcia. This untimely departure added sorrow to Felix's already grieving heart. Felix had to face the reality of bidding farewell to his beloved wife, a woman who had been his pillar of strength.

As the news of Louise Mathilde's passing spread, the friends and acquaintances of the Garcia family were called upon to join Felix in paying homage to his departed wife. The funeral arrangements were swiftly made, and the occasion was set to take place on the very same day, the 3rd of September, in the Parish of St. Charles. (New Orleans Bee 1852)

To facilitate the transportation of those who wished to bid their final farewells, a special arrangement was made. The steamboat Fashion, a vessel reserved exclusively for this purpose, awaited mourners at the foot of Jackson Street in the 4th District. Amidst a haze of grief, Felix and his fellow mourners sailed towards the Parish of St. Charles Borromeo

Church. As the steamboat ferried them across the waters, Felix found himself surrounded by a community united in grief.

In the aftermath of the crushing losses that befell Felix Garcia, his descent into hardship and adversity began. Desperate to clothe the slaves and conduct necessary repairs on the plantation, Felix turned to his brother-in-law and borrowed the sum of $5000. However, as fate would have it, another challenge emerged in the form of Christophe Strantz. Claiming to have worked as an overseer on Felix Garcia's plantation in the parish of St. Charles, Strantz attempted to collect a debt from Felix Garcia. Strantz claimed to have worked for the company from December 1848 until February 6, 1850, at an annual salary of $1,200 that had been agreed upon.

To secure payment for his services and expenses, Felix Garcia had signed a draft amounting to $1,866, to be drawn on P. Rotchford of New Orleans. But Strantz encountered resistance when he offered to pay for the conscription. Strantz continued to express his frustrations by claiming that 75 hogsheads of sugar, which he was entitled to as security for the debt, were being carried into the brig Detroit and were about to be exported from the state. Given these facts, Strantz attempted to establish his claim by requesting an order of sequestration for the seventy-five hogsheads of sugar. Furthermore, he claimed a $1,866 judgment against Felix Garcia, as well as recognition of his sugar shipment privilege. This legal entanglement compounded Felix Garcia's difficult path, as he became embroiled in financial issues and the potential loss of valuable assets. (Christophe Strantz 1850)

Beyond the conflicts with his brother-in-law, Felix faced legal troubles with his own brother, Carlos Garcia, as well. Carlos, who had been employed as an overseer on Felix's plantations, sued him for unpaid wages. As the case unfolded in the Supreme Court of

Louisiana, the details of the lawsuit revealed a complex financial situation. The core issue revolved around Carlos' wages as an overseer. He wasn't paid a fixed salary, which was the usual practice. Instead, he argued for a fair wage based on the value of his services, known as "quantum meruit". The court, however, found his initial claim of $1800 per year excessive. Examining the evidence, they determined a more reasonable wage to be $1200 annually, meaning Felix owed Carlos $400 in back pay. (Reports of Cases Argued and Determined in the Supreme Court of LA, Book 24 1852)

Unfortunately, things were further complicated due to an "antichresis" agreement Felix had made with Dunlop, Moncure & Company. An antichresis is a type of secured loan where the creditor takes possession of the debtor's property (in this case, the plantations) until the debt is repaid. However, the agreement stipulated that Felix would remain on the plantations as a manager. His spending authority was limited to $8000 per year, and he was obligated to purchase supplies through Dunlop, Moncure & Company.

The lawsuit revealed that Felix likely exceeded this spending limit during the plantation's management. Furthermore, Carlos, acting as an overseer, had authorized additional supplies and incurred expenses beyond the agreed-upon budget. He had personally paid for some of these expenses, but others remained outstanding. Dunlop, Moncure & Company, the antichresis creditors, contested Carlos' claims. They argued that his requested wages were outrageous and didn't qualify as a privilege on the crop - meaning they wouldn't be paid first before other debts. Additionally, they questioned whether some of the expenses Carlos claimed to have incurred ever actually happened.

The court ultimately ruled in favor of Carlos on the wage issue. They recognized his role as an overseer entitled him to a privilege on the crop for his unpaid wages. Furthermore, they established that Carlos' privilege extended to the supplies and expenses he had personally paid for, as these were necessary for the plantation's operation.

Consequently, this lawsuit exposed a web of financial difficulties Felix was facing. The limited budget imposed by the antichresis agreement might have hampered his ability to effectively manage the plantations. Additionally, exceeding the budget and relying on his brother to secure additional supplies suggests potential cash flow problems.

Felix Garcia's life, on the cusp of financial ruin, took an unexpected turn. In July 1853, a banquet was held in his honor in New Orleans, marking the beginning of his transformative expedition. The esteemed Mr. A. Baron Potet, a dear friend and old companion, penned a heartfelt message to Felix, bidding him farewell as he prepared to depart for Paris via Havana and New York City. (Dupotet 1853)

The voyage began aboard the Steamship Crescent City, carrying Felix across the tumultuous seas to Havana, where the ship encountered rough weather. Undeterred by the challenges, the journey continued, propelling Felix towards New York before finally leading him to the enchanting city of Paris. (Letter from Havana 1853)

France, the City of Lights, offered Felix a new environment, a chance to step away from the pressures of Louisiana. He settled in Ixelles, a commune within Paris, and it was here that he focused on his true passion - sugar refining. His invention, the soap-based method for clarifying sugar juice, hadn't reached its full potential back home. Now, in Paris, he had the opportunity to refine it further.

In September 1857, he secured a patent of development for additions to the manufacture of alcohols. These patents likely represented further refinements to his existing inventions, perhaps expanding their application beyond sugar to the production of alcohol.

The streets of Paris bore witness to Felix's tireless dedication, with Rue Rocherchouart serving as his address in early 1855 before his transition to 51 Rue Taitbout in December. These addresses offer a glimpse into his Parisian life, the streets he walked, the cafes he frequented. Unfortunately, such details remain a tantalizing glimpse into the past.

Amidst the bustling streets of Paris, Felix's groundbreaking work drew the attention of Mr. Basset, who addressed a theoretical and experimental report on the innovative use of soap. He deemed it as a more effective and economic means of defecating sugars. This revolutionary approach, championed by Felix, sought to address the inherent challenges of outdated methods. Traditionally, lime was used in this process, but it had drawbacks. Too little lime resulted in poorly purified juices, while too much led to a reduced sugar yield. Felix's soap solution offered a potential solution, promising clearer, purer juice with a higher sugar content.

The report details the process: after treatment with lime, the sugar juices were mixed with a soap solution, agitated, and brought to a boil. This resulted in the formation of scums that rose to the surface, leaving behind a clear, odorless liquid. The benefits went beyond simple clarification. The report claims that the soap-treated juices cooked and crystallized more easily, leading to a higher overall sugar yield.

This innovation wasn't just theoretical. Large-scale trials were conducted at the factory of the Bouzet brothers in Haubourdin. The results were positive, confirming the advantages outlined by Mr. Basset. The method was deemed economical as it required no special equipment and offered a higher sugar yield compared to traditional methods. Furthermore, Mr. Mene, a French chemist, discovered an application of hydrate of alumina for the same purpose, further solidifying the impact of Felix's visionary approach on the industry.

News of Felix's invention even reached across the Atlantic. An article in a Louisiana newspaper reported that "Mr. Garcia, a Louisiana sugar refiner, has brought before the academy of sciences at Paris, a process for clarifying sugar with soap." This recognition, while occurring far from home, must have brought a sense of vindication to Felix.

Felix Garcia's Parisian years were marked by both hope and hardship. While he tirelessly refined his sugar processing invention, his personal life faced significant challenges. Throughout these ordeals, Marie Aimée Garcia stood by her father's side in Paris. In 1857, Marie Aimée, burdened by the weight of financial strain, penned a distressing letter from Paris to their home in Louisiana. In her heartfelt plea, she requested the sale of her last remaining slave. Despite Felix's unwavering dedication to perfecting his patents for processing sugar, their hopes for financial stability remained unfulfilled.

The year 1859 brought a somber turn. Felix fell ill in December. Knowing his time was near, he made a final gesture of love for his illegitimate son, Charles. On his deathbed, he entrusted Marie Aimée with his watch and ring, requesting she pass them on to Charles. This act of remembrance, reaching across familial boundaries, speaks volumes about Felix's character.

Felix Garcia passed away on January 11th, 1859, at the age of 57. A Parisian newspaper, La Presse, noted his passing. He was initially entombed at the renowned Montmartre Cemetery in Paris. However, a year later, his remains were transferred to the city's catacombs, a final resting place shared by countless Parisians. (La Presse 1859) (Alpha Register Montmartre 1859)

Back in Louisiana, Felix's death wasn't met with silence. A eulogy delivered in the Senate paints a vivid picture of the man he was. The speaker, addressing the president, described Felix as "one of our most dearly beloved citizens," a man of "chivalric and high-toned character." He highlighted Felix's contributions to the state, calling him "one of her noblest children." The eulogy concluded with a motion to adjourn the Senate meeting as a mark of respect for Felix's memory. (Daily Advocate 1859)

Felix Garcia's story remains a compelling one. While his financial success remained elusive, his legacy extends beyond his inventions. He was a man of ambition and determination and a figure who commanded respect in his community. His journey from the bustling streets of New Orleans to the scientific salons of Paris highlights the human spirit's unyielding pursuit of innovation and the enduring power of will.

Chapter Five:
Manuel J. Garcia's Contributions

Manuel J. Garcia's name is a lineage carved deep into the heart of history. He wasn't a mere citizen; he was the architect of a sprawling family; he was a human cornerstone holding a multitude of lives together. His story isn't a chronicle of grand feats but a vibrant biography etched with the experiences of twenty-four children, out of which only five survived – a testament not to pride but to the sheer force of his love. This fact alone speaks volumes about the depth of his love - a love so profound it's rarely seen on this earth. He wasn't just a leader but a bulwark who withstood storms that would have broken lesser men. He was a provider, offering untiring support to those who chose to stand by him. He owed them nothing, but he offered his friends endless support nonetheless.

Manuel J. Garcia, a man of Spanish/French descent, was born in a place of cultural crossroads – New Orleans, Louisiana. He was born on November 13, 1795, on the corner of S. Pierre and Bourbon Street within the confines of family property. (New Orleans Bee 1884) His lineage boasted a history of honorable service; his father, a veteran of the Spanish Navy, captained the La Proserpine while stationed in New Orleans.

The winds of change, however, would soon alter the course of Manuel Garcia's life. When Louisiana ceded to French control, the Garcia family uprooted themselves, seeking new residence in Pensacola. Here, Manuel's father established himself in St. Jean-Baptiste Parish. (New Orleans Bee 1884)

Despite establishing roots in Pensacola, fate had another twist in store for Manuel Garcia. The War of 1812 erupted, disrupting the newly settled life for the Manuel Garcia family. The young Manuel, with the spirit of patriotism burning bright, couldn't stay idle. He answered the call to arms, eager to defend his adopted nation. His bravery found expression on the battlefield as he served in the regiment under Colonel Labranche. This dedication to his new homeland extended further with his documented participation in Major J. B. Plauché's Battalion d'Orléans, a unit of the Carabiniers, on December 20, 1814. This battalion was composed of the city's elite, primarily of French origin. (Holmes 1940)

Despite the youth and delicacy of many of its members, the battalion was renowned for its remarkable endurance and spirit. They bore their heavy muskets and knapsacks with the ease of seasoned veterans. Their distinctive and tasteful uniforms, bold countenances, and uniform size made them a formidable presence on the battlefield. Initially stationed at Spanish Fort, Manuel Garcia and his battalion were ordered to march to the Place d'Armas. According to legend, they covered the entire distance on foot in a swift dash. Upon their arrival, they joined the review of the troops by General Andrew Jackson.

After fulfilling his military duty, Manuel could focus on building his own family life. The war had undoubtedly left its mark, shaping him into a man of courage and resilience. These qualities, no doubt, served him well in the years to come. Years passed, filled with the quiet hum of building a life. Having established himself as a member of one of the most respected families in the state, a reputation likely bolstered by his wartime service, Manuel Garcia took a pivotal step. On December 27, 1822, he married the young Miss Eliza Fortier, embarking on a new chapter filled with the promise of love and family at the age of 27.

Manuel's life wasn't without its challenges. He extended his endeavors beyond the immediate family unit, establishing a small plantation for himself in Jefferson Parish. This venture into land ownership offered the potential for prosperity, but fate intervened. Disaster struck in March of 1830 when a fire ripped through his sugar house located in the Bonnet Carre area. The inferno not only consumed the sugar house but also spread to a nearby stable and several other outbuildings. This devastating event resulted in the loss of his entire sugar crop and likely some livestock as well. The financial toll was significant, forcing Manuel to seek a financial reorganization with his creditors, presumably the bank. (Sugar House Fire 1830)

Undeterred by the plantation setback, Manuel Garcia displayed his characteristic resilience. He broadened his horizons by entering the political arena. Perhaps his wartime service, his standing within the community, or a combination of both had established a reputation and influence that proved to be valuable assets. This foray into the political arena culminated in a significant achievement in 1836. The residents of Jefferson Parish elected him as their Sheriff. This appointment not only marked a shift in his career path but also served as a reflection of the public's trust in his leadership. The following nine years were marked by a consistent display of his proven abilities and unwavering integrity. As

Sheriff, Manuel Garcia would have shouldered a significant responsibility, ensuring law and order within the parish.

Manuel Garcia's political activism wasn't confined to his duties as Sheriff. In 1842, he joined forces with his brother, Felix, in a move that would have significant economic ramifications. Together, they signed a Sugar Tariff Petition addressed to the U.S. Congress. This petition wasn't simply an expression of opinion; it was a strategic maneuver aimed at protecting domestic sugar producers like themselves. The brothers argued for a tariff on imported sugar, a levy that would make foreign sugar more expensive and thus increase the demand and profitability of American-grown sugar. Their efforts, along with the lobbying efforts of others in the industry, proved successful. The U.S. Congress implemented a sugar import tariff, a policy that remains in place to this day. This victory undoubtedly solidified Manuel Garcia's reputation as a shrewd advocate for Louisiana's economic interests.

Manuel Garcia's political ambition extended beyond the local level. In 1845, he took a step that would place him on a larger political stage. He entered the Louisiana State Senate, representing the people of Jefferson Parish, his adopted home. This move signaled not only his own political aspirations but also the public's trust in his leadership abilities. Interestingly, he followed in the footsteps of his brother, Felix, by aligning himself with the Whig party. The Whigs were known for attracting prominent and respected individuals, and their focus on fiscal responsibility and limited government resonated with Manuel Garcia's own values. This political affiliation further cemented his image as a man of integrity and influence within the state.

Manuel Garcia's political career continued to flourish. He wasn't immune to the national political tides, however. In 1848, the country celebrated the presidential victory of Zachary Taylor, a Whig hero.

Manuel's alignment with the Whig party likely played a role in his own political fortunes that year. He was appointed to the position of naval officer - a role that utilized his leadership skills in a different setting. He served in this capacity for four years, until 1852.

Even as Manuel Garcia navigated the political landscape, personal matters demanded his attention. In 1860, he experienced the loss of his sister, Josephine. Her passing came with an unexpected outcome: she bequeathed to him a share of the Widow Massicot Plantation. He purchased the balance from the estate. It was a property she had inherited from their mother, Aimée Marie Massicot. This inheritance likely solidified Manuel's financial standing.

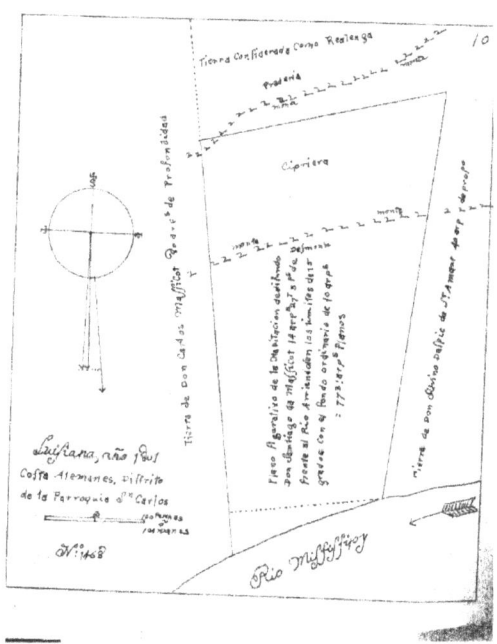

Survey map of the Widow Massicot plantation. Later Josephine's and then Manuel J. Garcia's plantation. From the Vicente Sebastián Pintado collection.

However, the nation was hurtling towards a tumultuous period at the time. The secession movement gained momentum, and Louisiana was caught in the throes of the debate. Manuel Garcia was a staunch Union supporter, but he found himself in a difficult position. While his personal beliefs aligned with the Union, he also held a deep respect for his adopted state, Louisiana. Ultimately, he chose a path of loyalty, prioritizing the will of the state over his own convictions. Given his advancing age, he opted to leave Louisiana rather than actively participate in the brewing conflict. With the arrival of federal troops in New Orleans, Manuel Garcia and his family relocated to Pensacola, Florida, where they remained for the duration of the Civil War. This decision reflected a complex blend of loyalty, pragmatism, and a desire to protect his family from the ravages of war.

While Manuel Garcia's contributions were widely respected, the Garcia family's public image was tested in the early 1890s with his son Eugene's involvement in a financial scandal. In the early 1890s, Eugene F. Garcia, once a respected paying teller at the Louisiana National Bank, found himself at the center of a high-profile financial scandal. This case began in October 1891 and continued into 1892, capturing widespread public attention. On October 23, 1891, the bank discovered a deficit of $190,000, a massive sum for the time. Eugene Garcia, as the paying teller, was directly implicated in this loss. This revelation cast a shadow over his previously unblemished career, suggesting possible embezzlement or gross financial mismanagement. (Daily Picayune 1892)

The next day, October 24, 1891, further details emerged about Eugene Garcia's predicament. He was arrested based on a warrant issued by the United States Commissioner. This indicated that federal authorities were involved, underscoring the seriousness of the charges against him. Despite the gravity of the situation, Eugene Garcia was released on a bond of $25,000. By February 16, 1892, Eugene Garcia was on trial.

On the first day of the trial, the courtroom was filled with onlookers eager to see how the case would unfold. The prosecution presented its case methodically, laying out evidence of the missing funds and highlighting Eugene Garcia's responsibilities as a paying teller. Witnesses were called to testify about the bank's operations and Garcia's actions in the days leading up to the discovery of the deficit. Eugene's defense team worked diligently to counter the prosecution's narrative. They questioned the reliability of the bank's records and suggested that other employees could have been responsible for the missing money. The defense aimed to cast doubt on the prosecution's evidence, arguing that it was insufficient to conclusively prove Eugene's guilt. Some saw Eugene Garcia as a victim of circumstance, potentially scapegoated for broader issues within the bank. Others viewed him as a cunning embezzler who betrayed the trust placed in him by his employers and the public. Eventually, Eugene Garcia was found not guilty.

Admittedly, there had been legal struggles prevalent within this family. However, historical accounts reveal that Manuel Garcia was a family man through and through. His dedication is revealed by a heartfelt letter sent to his brother, Carlos Garcia, in April of 1859. At the time, Manuel Garcia penned the message with a tremor caused by rheumatism. This physical ailment delayed Manuel's response to Carlos's earlier letter, but it couldn't dampen his spirit or his concern for his nephew. The opening lines revealed a deep empathy for Carlos's struggles: "My dear Carlos, I was not able to answer your letter of the 15th any sooner due to my rheumatism. I had been a bit improved over the past two or three days, but last night, I suffered in my arm and fingers." (Manuel to Carlos, April 24, 1859)

Manuel's empathy extended beyond his brother's physical ailments. He intuited the emotional toll of misfortune and isolation: "I had expected the pain which you are experiencing, as much because of the misfortunes which have overwhelmed you one after another, as the isolation to which you are reduced."

This passage hinted at the challenges Carlos faced, perhaps a difficult job location far from his family. Manuel's words showed a long-held desire for Carlos's return. He acknowledged a missed opportunity, perhaps a past disagreement that kept Carlos at a distance. The letter expressed regret:

"Let me assure you that I have often wanted to speak to you of the regrets I have felt in being obliged to be separated from you. Especially in these current circumstances, my tongue would become paralyzed as soon as I wanted to broach the subject."

This sentiment was followed by a clear invitation: "Be assured that I would have wanted something to happen that would have broken your engagement because (with) Felix and Josephine dead it was no longer urgent that you hire yourself on in a place so difficult and so far from yours (your family)."

The loss of Felix and Josephine, Manuel's brother and sister, seemingly removed any obligation Carlos might have felt to remain in his distant position. The letter emphasized the strong family bond, assuring Carlos, "We would have always gotten along and that my children regard you as a brother and a friend."

This sentiment wasn't just empty words. Manuel expressed a heartfelt desire for Carlos to rejoin the family unit: "I have never been able to speak to you of the desire that I have for you to live with us (Tu resseus de rester avec nous)." He wasn't alone in this wish. The letter added, "Eliza, who shares my hopes and desires, that I communicate them to you. Thus, if you do not find her in good health, come to rejoin us." Eliza, Manuel's wife, clearly echoed his yearning for a complete family circle.

The letter then shifted to updates on other family members. News of Josephine's grief over her sister's passing demonstrated the family's shared grief. Furthermore, he shared a more concerning update with news of Pamela's health: "Pamela is very sick. I do not believe that she can go much longer." The letter offered a mix of sorrow and hope. While some family members faced health challenges, others found reasons for optimism. Dolores's health seemed to be improving, with Manuel reporting that "Dolores has been rejuvenated."

Furthermore, the letter touched on the sale of silverware, hinting at potential financial considerations: "I sold the silverware (a la monnaie/marrine) except for a dozen small spoons and two stew spoons (larger, soup spoons, maybe) that Peter is taking by weight at the same price that you had sold that which belonged to our poor Josephine." While the exact reason for the sale remained unclear, it suggested a pragmatic approach to managing the household finances.

Moving on, Manuel mentioned the passing of Mr. Edmond "Fontaine" and F. Martin, followed by another concerning update of another family member's poor health. However, the most surprising revelation emerged in the latter part of the letter. Manuel described encountering a young man claiming to be Felix's illegitimate son: "Eight days ago, I was accosted by a young man of fourteen years who claimed to be the son of Felix. As he was in a hurry, I simply told him that Felix had never told me that he had a son, and that I would look into it (prendrais des informations)."

The young man had introduced himself as Charles Garcia, and his mother's name was mentioned as Magdalena Adrian. However, Manuel expressed skepticism about the claim, highlighting the existence of Felix's legitimate daughter, Aimée, who lacked resources. The letter reflected Manuel's concern for this young man but also his responsibility towards Felix's legitimate heir.

The ailments Manuel faced were evident in his closing remarks: "I can no longer hold my pen, so much do my hands hurt; I do not know if you will be able to make out my scrawls." Despite the discomfort, his desire for connection with Carlos persisted. He expressed a longing for news: "Write to me, give me a few details relative to (space) and the plantation/homestead/residence (habitation). Do you have a few good neighbors?"

This request for information painted a picture of Manuel's yearning to stay connected with Carlos's life, even in his distant location. The letter concluded with a warm embrace: "I embrace you with all my heart." This simple statement shows the depth of Manuel's affection for his nephew. News of Honoret's promotion to a position at the bank with a promising salary added a final touch of optimism.

In conclusion, if we take a peek at Manuel Garcia's interactions with his family as well as his public image, we can see a compelling portrait of a man who consistently earned the trust and respect of everyone in his life. From his early days answering the call to arms to his leadership as Sheriff and State Senator, Manuel Garcia's actions were marked by a strong sense of duty and unwavering integrity. Even his foray into the economic sphere demonstrated a commitment to safeguarding the interests of his community. His political affiliation with the Whigs further underscored his own values and principles.

This public image of integrity and dedication impeccably translated into his private life drawing a small pension from the War of 1812. After a long and distinguished career, Manuel Garcia made a conscious choice to prioritize his family. He retreated from the public eye, focusing on nurturing his loved ones and leaving behind a legacy of honorable conduct. His children undoubtedly benefited from his guidance and the strong moral compass he instilled in them.

While public appearances became less frequent in his later years, those who encountered Manuel Garcia in his twilight years likely carried away a vivid memory. His enduring spirit, borne from his Creole heritage, firm patriotism, deep affection for his family, and an almost boundless energy, left a lasting impression. He remained a man of depth and complexity, an echo of the life well-lived.

Chapter Six:
Charles Garcia's Journey

Life after his mother's passing took Charles down a new path. He traded his past for the patient craft of a cabinet maker, most likely starting as an apprentice. During this period, he rekindled his relationship with his sister Aimée, who had taken on the role of a school teacher. At the same time, Charles became deeply involved in the bustling life of New Orleans.

Dr. Charles Garcia. Collection from Charles Elliott Wayne (formerly Charles Wayne Garcia), late 1860s.

The war fever gripping New Orleans reached a crescendo in the spring of 1861. Newspapers overflowed with advertisements for military units, their calls to action echoing the city's rising fervor.

Charles, caught in the current, enlisted in April with the Beauregard Rifles, a newly formed unit in the city.

Their first official meeting buzzed with activity. Mr. John Freret was elected president, while Mr. W. Semmes became their acting secretary. The city itself pulsed with a frenetic energy as new companies materialized seemingly overnight. The tireless quartermaster's department scrambled to equip these burgeoning forces. Their priority was securing essential supplies like shoes, clothing, and other necessities.[1]

The Beauregard Rifles themselves embodied the diversity of New Orleans. J.S. Austin, a metal manufacturer, marched alongside J.W. Barnum, a dentist. Charles found himself surrounded by a fascinating mix of professions – C.D. Brown, a tobacco merchant, stood shoulder-to-shoulder with J.F. Brown, who ran a general store. Justin Casbergue brought his furniture store experience, while Thomas Donnelly offered his skills honed behind a bar. R.L. Hayman, a physician, balanced his duties with M.B. Healy, who ran a local grocery. Clerks like E.H. Hyde, Eugene Meslier, M. Prudhomme, A.W. Skardon, and John B. Tusson (who would later rise to sergeant) added their talents to the mix. Charles Rhodes, a customs inspector, found himself side-by-side with Charles Ruffier, a stonecutter. T.B. Smith, a shoemaker, served alongside L.A. Sauton, an accountant. Ambrose W. Skardon, who worked for commission merchant Alexander Norton, and James MacAulay rounded out their eclectic group. Surprisingly, a number of their comrades were even schoolboys from prominent New Orleans families.[2]

---

[1] "The Recruiting Service," Daily Picayune (New Orleans, LA), sec. The City, April 20, 1861.

[2] "The Crescent Regiment," Trenton State Gazette (Trenton, NJ), June 28, 1865.

In total, 178 men, including Charles, formed Company D. The unit itself bore several names – Beauregard's Rangers, Vienne's Rangers, or even Venerable's Rangers. Captain Jules Vienne, a 37-year-old veteran of the Mexican War and a clerk at the fourth district court, led their company. Adjutant Richard Venables stood by his side. While "Beauregard's Rangers" became the most common name, "Rifles" occasionally popped up, adding to the confusion. Extensive research confirmed that they were indeed part of the Beauregard Rangers, the official designation. It's important to note that other Confederate units also bore the name "Beauregard Rifles".

In the early days of the Beauregard Rifles, one notable meeting occurred on the evening of April 24, 1861, at their armory on 83 Magazine Street. This gathering saw the adoption of resolutions that expressed deep gratitude towards Isaac Bridge, Alexander Moses, and David J. Workum. These men had generously provided the Rifles with a spacious room to use as their armory, free of charge. As a token of their appreciation, the Rifles declared these benefactors honorary members. The secretary was tasked with sending copies of these resolutions to the gentlemen and ensuring their publication in the Picayune, the Crescent, and the Delta.

Throughout the scorching summer evenings of 1861, the Beauregard Rifles could often be seen drilling along the levee of the Mississippi River. The New Orleans Bee and other local newspapers regularly featured announcements about their activities and other military news. Initially, the regiment consisted of eight companies, including units like the Crescent City Guards and the Louisiana Guards. By November, the Beauregard Rifles had gained a reputation as an elite unit, prompting the McConnell family to host a celebratory party in their honor. Additional companies, such as the Orleans Cadets and the Sumter Rifles, later joined the regiment, expanding its ranks.

One Thursday evening, Captain Meslier led the Beauregard Rifles in a parade through the city's main streets. The unit's impressive turnout and disciplined display drew admiration from spectators. After completing the parade, the soldiers returned to their armory to store their weapons before heading to the home of Mr. and Mrs. McConnell at 458 Magazine Street. There, they were greeted warmly and enjoyed a night of lively social interaction.

Upon their arrival, the soldiers entered the parlor, which was crowded with visitors, and lined up. Both the entry hall and the balcony were packed. Numerous young women attended the event, distributing copies of Mrs. McConnell's quickstep, "A Tribute to Beauregard," which was written for the Rifles. The intention of the composition's proceeds was to provide assistance for the unit.

Mr. Otie presented the quickstep, delivering a brief speech, to which Captain Meslier responded with sincere thanks. Miss Laura McConnell, the youngest daughter of the hosts, played a charming role in the evening. Dressed in white and adorned with Confederate colors, the 14-year-old presented hand-crafted housewives - small sewing kits - to the soldiers. These gifts were made with care and love, and as she handed them over, she recited lines written by Mrs. A. M. Richards, adding a personal and emotional touch to the occasion. These lines were:

Dear friends, I tremble before such a crowd,

And if my voice should not seem very loud,

Please pardon and accept each little token,

As if the words that gave, were better spoken.

I scarcely dared to raise my wandering eyes,

And yet I feel so grateful spirit rise –

To see a sight so glittering and so grand,

As this brave, bright and valiant soldier band.

I come to bring a housewife as a gift,

And for a bachelor, Oh! What a gift!

It will supply your needles and your thread,

And never with a word of murmur said.

See! Should a ball through your coat sleeve go

And such there may be from the cruel foe,

You've thought to turn to your good Housewife these,

And she will every rent and seem repair.

For me, I never will bestow this hand

But on a brave defender of this land,

And I sure those others think so too –

Don't you, Miss Mary? You, and you and you?

Soldiers, may Heaven in every action guard you,

May sweet peace and mercy soon reward you,

And when you need a trifle just a think on,

Remember you must conquer Mr. Lincoln.

The Crescent Regiment was a distinguished militia unit formed in New Orleans in late 1861. Comprised of eight uniformed companies, the regiment elected its officers with Marshall J. Smith as Colonel, George P. McPheeters as Lieutenant Colonel, and A.W. Bosworth as Major. The regiment took pride in its preparedness and held regular drills, initially demonstrating their battalion maneuvers on the levee the following Thursday.[3] These drills typically occurred on Thursdays at the foot of Girod Street, with an alternate location at the Delachaise Grounds in bad weather and the alternate day being Saturday.

Situated in the Delachaise Faubourg area, the park was expansive, including four square blocks, and was bounded by Delachaise, Laurel, Foucher, and Tchoupitoulas Streets.[4]

On December 20th, 1861, the Crescent Regiment received its first official assignment. Ordered by Colonel Smith and Adjutant Richard Venables, the regiment assembled to escort the remains of Colonel Frank Terry, a Texan soldier killed in battle. The body had been transported by train and lay in state at City Hall. The regiment formed a line, marched to City Hall, and then escorted Colonel Terry's remains to the ferry for its final journey back to Texas. Notably, officers from various other militia corps joined the funeral procession in a display of respect.[5]

News articles also highlighted an opportunity for citizens to join the esteemed Crescent Regiment. General Beauregard had recently accepted the regiment's service for a 90-day period, and there were openings available. Emphasizing the caliber of the regiment and its members, the

---

[3] "The Crescent Regiment," Daily Picayune (New Orleans, LA), sec. Front Page, December 2, 1861.

[4] "Military Notices," Times-Picayune (New Orleans), February 2, 1862.

[5] "Honors to Col. B. Frank Terry," Daily Picayune (New Orleans, LA), December 23, 1861.

notice described them as "the finest individuals from the city." The call to action mentioned benefits like reimbursement for enlistment necessities, implying financial advantages for those who joined.[6]

A hush fell over the bustling streets of New Orleans as Colonel Marshall J. Smith issued an unusual order. On that crisp Sunday morning in December, the Crescent Regiment wouldn't be drilling on the levee. He directed them to Poydras Street on a Sunday morning. It wasn't for drills or musters but for a gathering of faith at Christ Church.[7]

Uniformed but unarmed, the regiment marched in a sea of blue, a sight that both surprised and united the early churchgoers. Loyal attendees, accustomed to their usual pews, cheerfully yielded their spots. The church swelled with a newfound sense of community, some even standing near the overflowing doors to accommodate the soldiers who filed within the central pews.

Inside, a powerful synergy filled the air. Reverend G.W. Stickney, a chaplain draped in the Confederate colors, joined forces with the church's presbyter. Their co-led service resonated deeply, a call to arms intertwined with a call to faith. The sermons, delivered with conviction, urged the soldiers to be both fierce warriors and steadfast Christians.

Then came Reverend Dr. Leacock, the rector. His voice, devoid of military commands, resonated with blessings. He acknowledged their noble cause, the unwavering commitment to their country that burned bright in their eyes. However, he gently reminded them of the Christian values that anchored them – values of compassion,

---

[6] "Classified Ad 2," Daily Picayune (New Orleans, LA), sec. Military News, March 1, 1862.

[7] "Classified Ad 2," Daily Picayune (New Orleans, LA), sec. Military, March 2, 1862.

forgiveness, and absolute faith in a higher power. Tears welled up in the eyes of both soldiers and congregation. It was a moment of shared vulnerability in the face of impending sacrifice.

Throughout the service, the regimental flag, a beautiful symbol of both war and faith, was prominently displayed beneath the pulpit. It wasn't just a battle standard; its vibrant colors seemed to absorb the sanctity of the day. As the regiment marched out, the flag fluttered proudly, carrying with it the blessings received and the spirit ignited within the house of God. The Crescent Regiment left Christ Church not just as a unit but as a band of believers.

The Crescent Regiment, a pioneer among New Orleans' volunteer forces, faced a critical moment. On March 7th, 1862, the Daily True Delta announced the imminent departure of eight companies for the Western theater of war. However, a shadow loomed – three companies remained understaffed. The urgency was palpable. The call to arms echoed through the city. The Confederate Guards, Companies BMG, the Twiggs Guards, and a large contingent of the Crescent itself were ordered to assemble at their armories.[8]

The article implored young men to step forward, to become "swords leaping from their scabbards." The language was electric, urging them to fill the ranks and prevent the need for further inspiration.

The inclusion of Mayfield's poem, "Follow, brave boys, follow!" was used as a powerful call to action.[9] Its martial imagery and rallying

---

[8] The Confederate Guards, Companies BMG, the Twiggs Guards, and a large contingent of the Crescent itself were ordered to assemble at their armories.

[9] "The Crescent Regiment," Daily True Delta (New Orleans, LA), March 7, 1862.

cry for glory painted a vivid picture of the battlefield and the potential for heroism.

Follow, brave boys, follow!

'Tis the rollcall of the drum,

And bright steel's ringing music

With its spirit-stirring hum

'Tis the tramp of armed columns,

Brace in front to drawing near,

And the rattle of the sabers,

In the scabbards we hear:

Follow follow to a man boys,

So bravely leading on!

There's glory to be won!

-Millie Mayfield-[10]

The afternoon of March 8th, 1862, pulsed with anticipation in the vicinity of the Jackson Railroad Depot. The air crackled with a mix of excitement and tearful goodbyes. The scene was one of intense interest, drawing in "thousands of men, women, and children" who thronged the streets. Their destination was the depot, where a special train awaited.

---

[10] "Follow, Boys! Follow!" Daily True Delta (New Orleans, LA), March 8, 1862.

This wasn't just any departure. It was the Crescent Regiment, a revolutionary force among New Orleans' volunteers, setting off for the seat of war. They weren't alone. Joining them were the fifth company of the Washington Artillery, led by Captain Hodgkin. These two forces formed the "left wing" of a larger contingent heading out.

Colonel Marshall J. Smith, the leader of the Crescent Regiment, must have felt the weight of the moment. He was about to lead his men, some in their newly issued uniforms. The men of the Crescent Regiment received their uniforms in a mere three days. It was eventually discovered, meanwhile, that not every company had gotten its uniforms in time for departure. The uniforms were carefully manufactured and provided a neat and elegant appearance. They were made of tough, durable gray material. Some companies experienced delays in acquiring their uniforms prior to embarking on their military missions, even with the quick manufacture.[11]

The crowd swarmed around the departing train cars, desperately attempting to connect with loved ones one last time. Tears mingled with the buoyant spirits of the soldiers. A starting tear here, a heartfelt farewell there. Despite the emotional goodbyes, these brave men showed an unwavering resolve. They were confident, ready to serve with honor and distinction.[12]

News traveled fast in those days. Telegraphic dispatches crackled with updates. By the following day, word reached the Times-Picayune from friends and families of the departed soldiers. These messages, dated late the previous day and the night before, brought a sense of relief. Both the artillery and the Crescent Regiment had arrived safely in Jackson and

---

[11] "Uniforms," Daily Delta (New Orleans, LA), March 9, 1862.

[12] "Off For The Seat Of War," Daily Picayune (New Orleans, LA), sec. Editorial Article 3, March 9, 1862.

Grand Junction, Tennessee. Their spirits remained high, which was a reflection of their eagerness to answer the call of duty.

Later, it turned out that The Crescent Regiment had initially traveled to Jackson, Tennessee. There, their commander met with General Beauregard, the Confederate military leader. New orders were issued, directing the regiment to establish their camp at Grand Junction.[13]

The Crescent Regiment, brimming with youthful enthusiasm, had answered General Beauregard's call. These young men, many leaving their studies behind, embodied the spirit of Louisiana's finest. They were a well-equipped force, 900 muskets strong, ready to prove their dedication to the cause. Their arrival in Jackson, Tennessee, on March 7th marked a turning point – they were no longer raw recruits but soldiers on the cusp of duty. Their prompt response and preparedness spoke volumes about their eagerness to serve under Beauregard's leadership.[14]

Barely three weeks into their deployment, the 21st Louisiana Crescent Regiment, under the command of Colonel M.J. Smith, received their first taste of action. As they returned from a reconnaissance mission that stretched towards the Tennessee River, they found out they weren't alone. A contingent of Colonel Kocsis's Alabama Cavalry bolstered their ranks as they ventured 10 miles deep into enemy territory. The mission pushed them to within a hair's breadth, just 3 miles from Licking Creek near Hamburg, Tennessee. Intelligence suggested a significant enemy presence in the area.

---

[13] "Washington Artillery and Crescents En Route," Times-Picayune (New Orleans, LA), March 11, 1862.

[14] "Arrived Jackson," Mobile Register (Mobile, AL), March 13, 1862.

The enemy wasn't the only challenge they faced. As the Crescent Regiment marched towards Licking Creek, their pickets reported the unmistakable beat of enemy drums echoing through the air. But the most formidable obstacle lay in the path itself. The roads were in a woeful state. Swamps and stretches of mud and water, reaching knee-deep in some places, turned their advance into a grueling feat. The poor conditions undoubtedly left the regiment weary and tested their mettle.

Meanwhile, near Corinth, Mississippi, a scene that was unlike the one in Tennessee was taking place. A New Orleans Delta reporter, fresh from the bustling camps surrounding the city, offered a surprising account. He had braced himself for the usual sights of wartime – a sprawl of camps, an abundance of military equipment, and perhaps the telltale signs of the greatest plagues: an overconsumption of whiskey. Instead, he encountered something quite unexpected: exceptional orderliness. Drunkenness seemed like a problem of the past, replaced by a sense of discipline that would have made any Southerner proud.

The reporter attributed this remarkable change to the leadership of General Bragg and Brigadier General Gladden. These officers, he declared, deserved the "eternal gratitude of the South" for their steadfast commitment to discipline. General Bragg's reforms, rigorously enforced by the vigilant Brigadier General Gladden (Commandant of the post), had banished the scourge of alcohol from the encampment. Any attempt to bring in whiskey was met with swift action. This strict enforcement was crucial in maintaining the army's honor and reputation, turning them into an unassailable force.

The winds of war seemed to be shifting near Corinth, Mississippi. A stark contrast emerged from the challenges faced by the Crescent Regiment. News reports indicated a decrease in the frequency of battles. It was a possible acknowledgment by the enemy of the considerable strength of Confederate forces in the area. The terrain itself played a significant role. The rough terrain and transportation challenges fueled speculation that the enemy might choose to change their course of action towards another quarter. The Mississippi River was considered a possible route, with a potential concentration of enemy forces along its banks.

Meanwhile, a flurry of high-level discussions took place at the same time. Generals Beauregard, Johnston, Polk, and Bragg were all reported to be engaged in consultations. Beauregard was on his way back to Jackson, while Johnston remained in Corinth. The report noted that General Polk appeared to be in fine spirits and that General Beauregard was in good health, which was an optimistic observation. A compliment to General Gladden's excellent form was also given to his magnificent brigade of five elite regiments.

The Crescent Regiment encamped just outside the town, offered a glimpse into the realities of soldierly life. These 90-day volunteers were not immune to the hardships of war. There were some who struggled with the harsh service and unappealing rations. However, a sense of respect for leadership prevailed. The soldiers planned to re-enlist for a 12-month service upon completion of their initial term. The regiment's frequent relocations (five in total) and demanding scouting duties were particularly challenging for new recruits. Nonetheless, the Crescent Regiment was trying to adapt to the difficulties of campaigning, with the potential to become a highly efficient unit in the coming days.[15]

---

[15] "Our Army At Corinth," Charleston Mercury (Charleston, SC), sec. News of the War, April 4, 1862.

News from the field painted a picture of a regiment undergoing a rapid transformation. Since departing New Orleans, the Crescent Regiment had been under heavy orders to strike their tents seven times. Regarded as well-seasoned, Captain Tarleton, Orderly Liam Nelson, and Privates Frank Green and William Holcomb of the Twiggs Guards were praised as among the best in the army. The way they changed from inexperienced recruits to seasoned veterans demonstrated the transformational impact of military experiences.[16]

After the journey by rail ended, many soldiers left their musical instruments and personal items behind. We could imagine Charles left his prized violin and copy of Les Misérables (in French of course) behind.

Furthermore, the Crescent Regiment played a crucial role in the Battle of Shiloh. The Battle of Shiloh, also known as the Battle of Pittsburg Landing, was a significant conflict in the Western Theater of the American Civil War. The battle took place on April 6 and 7, 1862, in southwestern Tennessee. The Confederate Army, under the leadership of Generals Albert Sidney Johnston and P.G.T. Beauregard, initiated a surprise attack on the Union Army, which was commanded by Major General Ulysses S. Grant. The primary objective of the Confederates was to defeat Grant's army before it could receive reinforcements from Major General Don Carlos Buell's Army of the Ohio.

The first day of the battle saw the Confederates achieving initial success, pushing the Union forces back towards the Tennessee River. However, the Union forces managed to establish a robust defensive line around a position known as "the Hornet's Nest." The second day

---

[16] Sparta, "From The Seat Of War," Daily Picayune (New Orleans, LA), sec. Special Correspondence, March 28, 1862.

of the battle witnessed a shift in momentum. With reinforcements from Buell's army, the Union forces launched a counterattack and regained the lost ground. This forced the Confederates to retreat, marking the end of the battle.

The Battle of Shiloh was one of the bloodiest battles in the Civil War, with approximately 23,746 casualties. Despite the heavy losses, it was a strategic victory for the Union, as it halted the Confederate advance in the Western Theater. The battle also marked the emergence of Ulysses S. Grant as a major figure in the Union war effort. His leadership during the battle played a crucial role in the Union's success and his subsequent rise in the ranks of the Union Army.

As part of the group that fought "its way through the Hornet's Nest" on April 6th, the Crescent Regiment bore the weight of a fierce battle. The human cost was significant, with the regiment suffering losses of 23 killed, 84 wounded and 20 missing. However, in Company D, Charles's unit, also known as the Beauregard Rangers, no one was found to be missing.

However, as General Bragg's Army evacuated Corinth, Mississippi, in 1862, a sobering reality emerged. Nearly a quarter of the soldiers were not fit for service due to illness. Captain S. R. Weston and the narrator, both from Company E of the Fifth Georgia Regiment, found themselves on the list of sick individuals. Though unfit for marching, they were assigned the critical duty of looking after the sick soldiers who would be transported on a separate train.

One day, a group of men were loading quartermaster and commissary goods onto a train at the depot. There was confusion in the air and everyone was moving quickly, making for a chaotic situation. All the physically fit stragglers were assigned tasks, and many of the ill were forced to help even if they needed to recover.

A young soldier, tall and handsome, albeit pale and petite, made his way toward the train reserved for the sick. The overseer of the work squad, spotting him, shouted, "Hey, young man, fall in here and get to work! Load these goods onto the cars, and be quick about it!"

This young soldier was none other than Charles Garcia. He looked the overseer in the eye and responded, "I'm not able to work. If I were, I would be with my company."

Growing irritated by Charles's response, the overseer yelled back, "Eh, won't work? We'll see about that. General!"

Leaving Charles alone momentarily, he walked away only to call General Bragg. Approaching the general, he told on Charles. "That man is refusing to work," he said and pointed towards Charles.

General Bragg paused and locked his stare on the young man, his eyes flashing with intensity. He reiterated the command for Charles to assist in loading the freight all at once. Charles, unimpressed, stayed firm and repeated his previous stance, stating that he was unable to work. If he were fit to labor, he would join his company and march and battle alongside them.

General Bragg's eyes seemed to crackle with fury as he roared, "What? You dare disobey my orders?"

Charles stood firm in his conviction and replied calmly, "I do."

General Bragg was visibly fuming and wasted no time. He barked an order at a Lieutenant overseeing a company of Louisiana regulars on guard duty. "Take a firing squad," he bellowed, "and escort this man to the grove. Shoot him!"

The Lieutenant, clearly surprised by the harsh command, scrambled to obey. He called upon six of his most reliable men and ordered them to lower their muskets. As they complied, General Bragg beckoned the Lieutenant aside. They retreated behind a nearby garden wall. Whatever transpired there seemingly altered the course of events. General Bragg walked away, and the Lieutenant, his demeanor transformed, marched Charles towards a grove situated about a hundred yards to our right.

Beneath the sprawling branches of a large oak, Charles was positioned on a stool. The guards, following protocol, attempted to blindfold him. However, Charles refused this indignity. Instead, with a quiet composure that belied the gravity of the situation, he removed his precious belongings: a gold watch and chain, along with a gold ring adorning his finger. He entrusted these keepsakes to the Lieutenant. In a steady voice, he requested they be delivered to his sister. Taking a scrap of paper, he carefully wrote her name and address, ensuring these final wishes were fulfilled. Returning to his position against the tree, a remarkable display of courage etched on his face, Charles uttered with a "proud smile upon his lips and without a tremor in his voice," the simple words, "Now, sir, I am ready."

The tension reached a breaking point. The Lieutenant retreated ten paces and positioned his men. A piercing command, clearly audible even from our distance, tore through the air: "Ready! Aim!"

There sat Private Garcia, as he was known, staring down the barrels of muskets aimed directly at his heart, any one of which could extinguish his life in an instant. Charles, however, remained composed as if posing for a portrait.

But then, in a startling turn of events, the Lieutenant issued another command: "Recover arms!" The men, visibly relieved, lowered their weapons with haste. The Lieutenant approached Charles, no longer a figure of authority but one filled with a newfound respect. He requested Charles to stand and, in a gesture of surprising amity, shook his hand with admiration. He then returned the watch, chain, and ring. Charles, accepting his belongings with a polite bow and a simple "Thanks," turned and walked away, seemingly unfazed by the brush with death he had just experienced. It was as if nothing extraordinary had transpired.

The Lieutenant and his men returned to their post. Moments later, General Bragg reappeared, and his earlier anger had seemingly dissipated. He inquired, "Where is the boy?"

"Gone," responded the Lieutenant simply.

General Bragg's next question hung heavy in the air: "What did you do?"

"Just exactly as you directed," he replied to General Bragg. He recounted the events in detail – Charles handing over his valuables for his sister (Aimée Garcia), taking his position with surprising resolve, refusing the blindfold, and facing the firing squad with bold courage. As he explained, the Lieutenant's eyes welled with tears.

General Bragg's demeanor was also noticeably altered. He demanded, "Who is he and where is he?" His voice now held a newfound urgency, a stark contrast to his earlier anger. He scanned the area, searching for the young soldier who had faced death with such dignity.

"I don't know," admitted the Lieutenant. He then offered a glimmer of hope, pulling out a scrap of paper with Aimée Garcia's address. "Here's his sister's name and address," he said, handing it to the General.

General Bragg took the paper. He pocketed it and declared, "Well, I'll find him and promote him!" With renewed purpose, he set off in search of this young hero.

The order to execute Charles had likely reached the ears of a hundred soldiers. In the face of such a chilling command, chaos erupted. Some scurried back to their assigned duties, seeking normalcy amidst the turmoil. Others sought refuge. A select few, including Captain Weston and perhaps a handful of others, remained transfixed, witnessing the entire ordeal unfold.

The aftermath was shrouded in a veil of misinformation. Many soldiers believed General Bragg had ordered Charles' execution. The General's reputation as a strict disciplinarian fueled these rumors. However, this incident offered a glimpse into a complexity perhaps hidden beneath the surface – a man known for his harshness might possess a well of compassion unseen by many.

Years later, Charles Garcia, after practicing medicine, stepped forward himself, confirming his identity as the young soldier who stared down death. Settling into his office chair on Chouteau Avenue after a long night tending to a demanding patient, he reflected on his wartime experiences. "I closed the book of the war years ago," he admitted. The memories, he confessed, held "so much that is unpleasant and bitter" that revisiting them was a burden he rarely chose to bear. Despite that, a spark of interest ignited when he encountered the "Recorder" story detailing his ordeal. "It was quite correct as to the features of the incident," he acknowledged.

NE Corner of Chouteau Avenue and 13th Street, St. Louis, MO. Compton, Richard J., and Camille N. Dry. Pictorial St. Louis, the great metropolis of the Mississippi valley; a topographical survey drawn in perspective A.D. St. Louis: Compton & Co., 1876.

A gentle plea hung in the air: "Won't you tell the story again?"

Reminiscing about the past, Charles Garcia recounted his enlistment with the Beauregard Rifles, a company within the Crescent Regiment from New Orleans. He described the retreat to Corinth following the Battle of Shiloh and the subsequent demonstration to mask the Confederate Army's true objective – a retreat to Tupelo. It was during this period of upheaval that illness struck him down. Camp fever left him weak and desperate for medical attention. Unable to locate a surgeon in the midst of uncertainty, he made his way to the train, hoping to find both a doctor and transportation. Charles, convinced he was too weak to walk the distance to Tupelo with his regiment, found himself apprehended, facing a potential death sentence in a secluded grove.

When Dr. Charles Garcia was asked what his sensations were while waiting for the command of "Fire," his response reflected his feelings of quiet resignation. "I can hardly tell," he confessed. He spoke of numbness that washes over a man who has faced danger before, a sense of acceptance as one prepares to meet their fate. Having already stared death in the face during battles like Shiloh, a certain level of detachment had set in. He simply "resigned himself."

The aftermath of the near-execution left Dr. Charles Garcia, then a young soldier, grappling with a mix of disbelief and newfound strength. He recounted, "I had not the least doubt in the world that I was standing there to be killed." Facing the muzzles of muskets aimed directly at him, he instinctively took what he believed to be his last breath. When the Lieutenant ordered the men to stand down, the sudden reprieve left him bewildered. "I could not understand why I was not dead," he admitted.

As soon as his ordeal ended, Charles wasted no time in leaving the scene. The sheer outrage of the situation, coupled with the fear that had gripped him, acted as a potent cure for his illness. He described feeling "strong and well," rejoining his company and marching all the way to Tupelo without a single relapse.

Fate, however, had a curious way of weaving its magic. Years later, Charles Garcia recounted, "I saw General Bragg at Tupelo."

This encounter took place while Charles' unit, the Beauregard Rifles, served as guards for General Beauregard. Detailed to guard General Bragg's headquarters, Charles found himself inadvertently forgotten during a routine shift change. He remained at his post until morning, exhaustion finally claiming him. Unable to find a comfortable spot to rest, he resorted to stacking bricks against a tree, creating a makeshift seat that maintained the illusion of him standing guard. It was in this precarious position that General Beauregard found him.

General Beauregard gently roused the sleeping soldier. "My son," he began, "you should not sleep on duty. If General Bragg had seen you, he would have shot you. Are you very tired?" Learning that Charles had been forgotten by the relief party, Beauregard offered him a reprieve from the rain. He instructed Charles to move to the porch, suggesting it offered an equally effective vantage point for guarding the post.

Moments later, General Bragg himself emerged. His booming voice demanded, "Where is the guard?"

Standing at the edge of the porch, Charles presented arms in a salute. However, his response to General Bragg's inquiry about his position was succinct: "General Beauregard told me to stand here, out of the rain."

This simple explanation triggered an eruption of anger from General Bragg. He launched into a tirade, spewing profanities aimed at Beauregard and other generals. He accused them of "making paper soldiers" of his men, claiming his position as second-in-command rendered him powerless to stop them.

Thankfully, Charles remained unrecognized. Knowing his place as a private soldier and unwilling to draw attention to himself, he held his silence. The encounter solidified his impression of General Bragg as "a martinet," a strict disciplinarian with a propensity for harsh punishments. Charles had personally witnessed the execution of three deserters on General Bragg's orders.

While Bragg was known for his severity and brutality, General Beauregard earned the respect and affection of his soldiers, constantly referring to them as "my sons and my boys." Charles never encountered General Bragg again after their brief, tense exchange at Tupelo.[17]

Charles spent the balance of the war as a guard for General Beauregard. In fact, Beauregard commandeered other soldiers from the Crescent Regiment and in particular the Beauregard Rangers for guard duty.

This unexpected encounter adds another layer to Charles Garcia's remarkable story. It provides a glimpse into the contrasting personalities of the two generals under whom he served, highlighting the complexities of leadership during wartime. More importantly, it serves as a reflection of Charles Garcia's own courage and resilience – a young soldier who stared down death and emerged a stronger, more determined man.

---

[17] "Ordered Shot: Dr. Charles Garcia's Experience At The Wrong End Of A Musket," St. Louis Post-Dispatch (St. Louis, MO), sec. Page 2, July 7, 1887.

Chapter Seven:
The Connallin Connection

John Connallin hailed from Bullaun, a quaint village nestled beside Loughrea in County Galway, Ireland. Born in 1836, his youth unfolded amidst the emerald pastures and rolling hills of the Irish countryside. Yet, by 1856, a yearning for a different life flickered within him. The whispers of opportunity across the Atlantic proved irresistible. With his brother Martin by his side, John set sail for America, a land brimming with promise. (Ft. Scott Daily Monitor 1898)

New York City was their first encounter with the new world. The sheer scale and dynamism of the city must have been a world apart from their quiet Irish village. Yet, the brothers weren't destined for the clamor of the city. Their hearts longed for open spaces and fresh beginnings. So, they pressed on westward, eventually settling in St. Louis.

John's life wasn't all tranquil pastures and fresh beginnings in the years leading up to the Civil War. He served in the militia, a local citizen's defense force. This wasn't some ceremonial duty station – his unit was deployed to Fort Scott, Kansas, a frontier outpost where tensions between pro-slavery and anti-slavery factions were exploding into violence. The year was 1856, and the seeds of the coming national conflict were already being sown on the bloody Kansas plains.

By 1858, the situation in southeast Kansas had deteriorated further. The territory had become a magnet for extremists on both sides of the slavery debate, energized by growing unrest elsewhere in the nation. James Montgomery, a fiery abolitionist, became a prominent figure among the free-state forces and was linked to a string of violent incidents. John found himself in the heart of this chaos, a firsthand witness to the escalating tensions.

The year 1858 saw Kansas erupt in violence. In April, John may have been part of the U.S. troops stationed at Fort Scott when they clashed with James Montgomery's free-state raiders at Paint Creek, a skirmish that left one soldier dead. Tensions continued to simmer, and by May, Montgomery's forces drove out pro-slavery elements from Linn County. This victory was tragically marred by the Marais des Cygnes Massacre, where eleven innocent free-staters were murdered. Rumors swirled that the attack was planned in the Western Hotel, further inflaming the animosity. As June dawned, Montgomery's men, fueled by anger and vengeance, attempted to burn down the very hotel believed to be the center of the pro-slavery conspiracy.

John was likely no stranger to the brutality erupting around him. However, military life, with its rigid discipline, proved a poor fit for his temperament. The Irishman possessed a fondness for whiskey, cheating at cards, and the thrill of gambling - vices that often landed him in hot water. Disillusioned and restless, John decided to call it quits on soldiery. He set his sights on St. Louis, where he planned to reunite with his family – parents William and Margaret, along with his siblings: brothers, Malachy, James, Joseph, and Patrick, and his sister Margaret Mary (Maggie) Connallin.

The tide of emigration had already swept many from County Galway across the Atlantic by the time the Connallin family set sail. The Irish countryside, once lush and verdant, bore the scars of absentee English landlords who prioritized their own gain over the well-being of their tenants. The Great Famine had come and gone, leaving a trail of devastation in its wake. It was under these circumstances that the Connallins, yearning for a life of opportunity, decided to join the exodus westward.

Exactly how they reached America remains a mystery, shrouded in the fog of time and the whimsical twists of family lore. Perhaps they landed in Boston, a bustling port city teeming with newcomers. Or maybe they disembarked in the vibrant chaos of New York City. There's even a family tale suggesting they sailed up the Mississippi River from New Orleans. One thing is certain: their journey was far from easy. Another intriguing story hints at a wilder journey – one of the brothers' meeting being thrown overboard for cheating at a card game. With the family name misspelled in various records, the truth may forever be lost.

What remains of the accounts reveals that John wasn't the only Connallin brother with a taste for adventure. They escaped being drafted for the Union or the Confederate cause because they were not citizens of the United States at the time.

However, joining their father William, brothers Joseph, Martin, and Patrick embarked on a new venture in St. Louis – the Legal Tender Saloon, situated on the bustling corner of 6th and Chestnut. While three of the brothers resided at 406 Cerre Street, just a stone's throw from where Busch Stadium stands today, their business catered to a different kind of crowd. With the Civil War raging, the Connallins saw an opportunity – supplying whiskey to soldiers on both sides of the conflict. It was a lucrative yet precarious enterprise, existing outside the law.

406 Cerre St. in St. Louis. Home of the Connallins and office of Dr. Charles Garcia. Compton, Richard J., and Camille N. Dry. Pictorial St. Louis, the great metropolis of the Mississippi valley; a topographical survey drawn in perspective A.D. St. Louis: Compton & Co., 1876.

This became especially clear when Patrick, caught running whiskey to soldiers, found himself on probation and needing court permission to travel between Kansas and St. Louis after the war. Patrick H. Connallin was a man of ambition and perhaps a hint of defiance. He ran the "Patrick H Connallin Saloon" on the prominent corner of 6th and Chestnut, likely drawing a lively crowd. Meanwhile, Joseph W. Connallin, a brother, served as his bartender.

However, beneath the surface of Patrick's business success lurked a past entanglement with the law. In 1865, he requested an extension of his parole. It seems his business required travel across state lines, and his parole restricted his movement. Further documents reveal a pledge from Patrick not to discuss a conversation with the Provost Marshal, a military official responsible for enforcing order. This suggests Patrick may have spilled some secrets in exchange for leniency. (Provost Marshal 1865)

As Patrick was getting in legal troubles, John followed in his brother's footsteps. During his early years in St. Louis, John found himself in the midst of a tumultuous period marked by conflicts over gambling establishments. According to a report from the St. Louis Democrat, the local police were engaged in an ongoing battle against these gambling houses. Despite facing resistance from the proprietors, who were low on ammunition and resources, the police continued their efforts to shut down these operations. (Flake's Bulletin 1868)

Captain Kohlhund led a series of raids, one of which included an incident on Fourth Street. There, the raiders, including Sergeant Gore and Con Duffy, stormed a notorious gambling house. As they approached, John's brother, Martin Connallin, attempted to warn the gamblers of the police's arrival by shouting "Police!" Martin was quickly apprehended and charged with vagrancy.

Duffy forcefully broke through the doors with his ax, allowing the raiding party to enter. Inside, they found evidence of the gamblers' hasty departure - overturned chairs, scattered chips, and a small amount of money left behind. Although most of the gamblers had escaped through a secret passage, the police captured a few individuals, including two young men from the country and two African American men.

The raiders continued their crackdown, targeting another keno house at the corner of Fourth and Elm. In this raid, they captured about twenty gamblers and seized the cheaply made furniture and gambling implements. Captain Kohlhund declared the keno operation "correct" and ordered the gamblers to remain seated. Despite the confiscation of their equipment, the value of the items was minimal, and the gamblers likely resumed their activities soon after.

As John wasn't exactly enamored with military discipline, his time in the Kansas Territory stationed at Fort Scott left a lasting impression. Perhaps it was the wide-open spaces or the burgeoning town itself, but John fell in love with the place during the border troubles. This fondness later influenced his decision to relocate there. John, along with his brothers James and Martin, eventually made the move to Fort Scott.

Life in Fort Scott brought more than just a change of scenery for John. There, he met Georgiana Singley, a captivating woman from Kentucky who charmed audiences with her singing and dancing talents. Georgiana, an accomplished performer who toured the Midwest, brought a touch of glamor to John's life. At once, their love blossomed, and they were married. Their family soon grew. In 1873, John Jr. arrived, and five years later, Georgiana gave birth to a daughter, Mary. However, as we'll see later, John's relationship with Mary would become a source of contention. John's marriage took a turn for the worse as well. (US Census 1880)

In 1881, John Connallin found himself embroiled in a dramatic and scandalous legal affair that captured public attention. John, apparently fueled by evidence of this bigamy, embarked on a determined pursuit of Georgiana and her alleged accomplice. The chase stretched across several cities – St. Louis, Kentucky, and finally, Chicago. This sudden departure was linked to a sensational case involving Octave Bouscaren, who had hastily married John's wife. Bouscaren was now facing trial on charges of perjury and bigamy, as he had deceitfully married John's wife. (The Evening Star 1882)

The legal proceedings revealed a tangled web of deceit and hasty decisions. Bouscaren's bond was set at $1,800, a substantial amount for the time, and he had been promptly arrested and jailed. His initial request for release on bond was denied when it was discovered that a prison warden had improperly issued the bond. This turn of events led to a broader investigation and scrutiny of the prison warden's actions.

John Connallin's involvement in the affair extended beyond his personal connections. He was charged with arranging the bond for his wife's new husband, Bouscaren, a move that was seen as controversial and possibly illegal. This action further complicated John's life and added to the public spectacle surrounding the case.

Apparently, Georgiana, black-haired, even went as far as disguising herself in a blonde wig to avoid detection. However, when she was caught red-handed, she was the very picture of weak-minded misery.

In a dramatic and emotionally charged courtroom event, John Connallin found himself face to face with a personal and public crisis. His estranged wife, overwhelmed by sorrow, moaned, "My God, what can I do!" as tears streamed down her face. Her body swayed, her voice choked with sobs, and she kept moaning incoherently, uttering words that sounded like "Mercy, mercy." It was a surreal sight, an actress giving in to genuine sorrow in such a theatrical manner that it paradoxically lessened the impact of her grief on the observers.

Standing beside her was Octave Bouscaren, her lover, who appeared calm and composed. However, the repeated sobs of his companion seemed to affect him, and his eyes reddened momentarily as he took his hand away from hers. Next to Bouscaren stood John Connallin, the deserted husband. John's reddish face, short gray hair, gray mustache, and imperial contrasted sharply with Bouscaren's youthful appearance. Bouscaren, scarcely more than 28, had a black beard and olive skin, with a melancholy expression that added to the tension of the scene.

At the request of the officers, the judge postponed the case to a later date to allow time for the necessary requisition papers. When the question of bail arose, John, who had maintained a collected and determined demeanor throughout, addressed the court. "This is a very exaggerated case, your honor. And you cannot place the bonds too high."

The court then turned to John's wife, asking for her statement. She halted her hysterical outburst and gasped, "Oh, I was driven to it. That man is a professional gambler. He has beaten me, and I have felt hunger and cold a hundred times. He made life intolerable to me, and I could bear it no longer." She continued in disjointed words to describe an outrage that John had allegedly perpetrated upon her when she was ill, but she soon broke down again, falling into another convulsive fit of weeping. Mr. Bouscaren, showing consideration, picked up a vial that had fallen from her hands and urged her to take her medicine.

In the courtroom, Mr. Bouscaren listened as the judge read the statute covering bigamy and suggested that the bail be set at $1,000. Drawing on his experience practicing law in Missouri, Mr. Bouscaren outlined the penalties associated with the crime. However, the judge ultimately fixed the bail at $3,000 in cash for each accused, leading to both John's estranged wife and Octave Bouscaren being taken to separate cells.

Shortly afterward, a reporter visited Mrs. Connallin in her cell, finding her still in the throes of hysteria. Despite her fine features and attractive appearance, she appeared utterly devoid of self-control and judgment, resembling a child in her emotional state. Tearfully, she began to recount her story, finding some relief in sharing her ordeal.

"I will tell you all about it," she said. "I married Mr. Connallin ten years ago in Kansas City. We have had five children, and two are now living. For eight years, he abused me continually. We lived for a while at Fort Scott, Kansas, where his persecutions continued. Judge Stewart of Kansas City can attest to my suffering, as he once drew up a bill of divorce for me. Mr. Curtis, of the Metropolitan Hotel, knows that Mr. Connallin has beaten me repeatedly. My husband was a gambler, often spending nights in debauchery and then coming to my room to beat me. I forgave him countless times and even concealed him when the police were after him in Kansas City. (In a Bad Plight 1882)

He accused me of infidelity, and while I was staying at the Metropolitan Hotel last June, he claimed I was criminally intimate with Mr. Bouscaren. When Mr. Bouscaren heard this, he said he would prove his honorable intentions by marrying me. I sought advice from a lady friend, and she said, 'Of course, marry him and show that gambler you can marry someone else.' I left Kansas City on June 19 and went to my mother's house in St. Louis. From there, I went to Mexico, Missouri, where Mr. Bouscaren joined me, and we were married on June 29. We moved to Chicago and have lived quietly ever since."

The courtroom drama surrounding John Connallin took another twist, with his wife's painful experiences coming to light. Terrified at the prospect of spending the night in the station, Mrs. Connallin revealed that she had a brother named Jesse Singley living in the area, hoping he could assist her. She confirmed her husband's claim that she had traveled for nearly two years with the Maggie Mitchell troupe, reflecting her talents as a vocalist. She produced notices from Kansas City papers that praised her performances at charity concerts, referring to her as Mrs. Georgie Connallin. She explained that for several months before her departure, she had been living alone at the Metropolitan Hotel, refusing to cohabit with her husband. Following her flight, she applied for a divorce, a suit that was still pending. She mentioned her son was at school in Holdbrook, and she had taken her little girl with her. The mention of her children threw her back into an agitated state, rendering her unable to continue her fragmented statement. Meanwhile, the reporter noted Octave Bouscaren in his cell, reclining on a bench with a melancholy demeanor akin to Hamlet. As a lawyer, Bouscaren maintained his professional secrecy, offering no statement when asked.

During the Civil War years of 1862-64, Georgie, along with her mother Mrs. Singley and her gambler brother Isaac, resided in a brick house. She was a striking young woman with a fine figure and brunette complexion and was known for her conspicuous presence on the streets, often dressed in a blue double-breasted sacque with brass buttons and brigadier general's straps on her shoulders, earning her the nickname "Brigadier."

Georgie and her mother solicited money from merchants and businessmen in Cincinnati and neighboring cities under the false pretense that the funds would aid the sick and wounded of the Union army. They amassed considerable sums and lived lavishly on the proceeds. Her beauty and supposed high rank attracted many young men of the time, many of whom later settled into respectable lives with families. After the war, Georgie disappeared from the public eye until her recent arrest brought her past back into the spotlight. The real facts remain unknown. However, John's past was marked by tremendous emotional conflicts and public scrutiny throughout this time.

Eventually, the circumstances became even more grim for John. In the early morning hours of Sunday, June 21, 1891, a tragic event unfolded in Fort Scott that would leave the community in mourning. The heavy rains from the previous day had caused a large dam to break, flooding the bottomlands and sweeping away houses like straws. This catastrophic event struck what was known as Buckrun's Bottom, spreading floodwaters over a mile wide. Many men, women, and children were left stranded on rooftops and in trees, visible but unreachable by spectators. (Daily Picayune 1891)

Among the heroes of that fateful day was John Connallin, Jr., the only child of John Connallin, a young man of admirable character and courage. During the storm and subsequent overflow, a rescue party braved the treacherous conditions to save those in danger. However, they were soon compelled to abandon their boat due to the rising waters. Many in the party managed to save their lives by clinging to trees, but John Connallin, Jr., aged 19, was not so fortunate. While attempting to hold onto a limb, it broke, and he was tragically swept away by the relentless current.

From dawn until afternoon, friends and rescuers scoured the muddy waters in a desperate search for his body, but their efforts were in vain. Despite firing numerous heavy blasts of dynamite over the water to bring his body to the surface, their attempts were unsuccessful. The body had not been submerged long enough for decomposition gases to make it buoyant, and it was likely not in the area being searched.

The last sighting of John, Jr. was in the treacherous current drawn through the narrow arches of the culverts with tremendous force. He likely rose and sank multiple times before succumbing to the waters, each time being pulled further towards the deadly vortex. It is believed that he continued to swim and struggle to escape the current until he was drawn under the arch and struck against the stones, eventually sinking into a deeper part of the stream where his body lay hidden.

The death of John Connallin, Jr. was profoundly heartbreaking. He was a young man of good character, well-liked by those who knew him. His father, John Connallin, Sr., was justly proud of his son and deeply attached to him. Friends and fellow members of the hose companies, who knew John, Jr. as a pleasant and reliable companion, felt the gravity of the situation deeply and made every effort to recover his body from the treacherous waters.

The floodwaters that ravaged Fort Scott began to recede on the night of June 21st, 1891. As the Marmaton River subsided, revealing the land it had submerged, a glimmer of hope flickered for those searching for John Connallin Jr. The moonlight illuminated the path for determined search parties, drawn by the reward offered in the previous day's papers. Among them were E.S. Goucher and Jap Coberly, who started a systematic search in the early hours of the morning. Their persistence paid off. In a low-lying area near Morton Well on Second Street, they discovered John Jr.'s body. The remains were transported to the Goodlander Funeral Supply Company, where undertakers prepared the body for viewing. Due to the time spent in the water, it was challenging to prepare the body. John Jr.'s face was discolored, but the undertakers managed to restore some semblance of normalcy. Embalming efforts were hampered by the state of the body, making the injection of fluids ineffective. Despite the ordeal, John Jr.'s body was recovered.

The recovered body of John Connallin Jr. offered a glimpse into the possible cause of his tragic demise. A severe injury to the skull, a crushed cerebellum on the right side, was most likely fatal. The left side also showed signs of significant bruising. Despite being a strong swimmer, John Jr. was likely no match for the raging current. Most probably, he was caught in the current's grip, unable to escape. The rushing water may have swept him towards the Third Street culvert, a point where the water formed a perilous whirlpool. Hurled against the unforgiving stonework by the swirling current, he likely sustained the fatal head injury. Rendered unconscious, he was then swept away by the torrent, his life extinguished in a matter of moments.

After being recovered, his body was prepared for transport to St. Louis for burial, accompanied by his grief-stricken father on the Missouri Pacific train. News of the tragedy reached John Jr.'s mother, Georgia Connallin, now residing in Omaha, through telegrams and news reports. Eighteen years old at the time of his death, John Jr. is remembered as a kind and helpful young man, a social individual known for his honesty and integrity. While no longer a member of Hose Company No. 2, his brief stint as a firefighter speaks to his selfless spirit. (Topeka Weekly 1891)

Adding to the sorrow, John, Jr. was beloved by his father, whose heart broke with anguish at his loss. The Connallin family, already marked by various trials and public scrutiny, now faced unimaginable grief. John Connallin, Sr. had to endure the profound sorrow of losing his only child, a promising young man who met a heroic yet tragic end.

Ultimately, the emotional blow proved to be too much for John Connallin. He breathed his last on a Tuesday night, March 10th, 1898. The fruit dealer and confectioner passed away at his sister's residence in St. Louis, where he had sought treatment for a chronic heart condition. News of his death came as a shock to the community, despite whispers of his declining health. His brother, James F. Connallin, who managed John's business, received a telegram simply stating the passing, devoid of details. A recent postcard from his nephew had hinted at John's precarious condition, but his imminent demise was unexpected. The report attributed the cause of death to chronic stomach issues that had plagued John for years, ultimately impacting his heart. While his passing was anticipated by close family, it came as a surprise to the wider community.

John's health had been on a downward spiral ever since the tragic loss of his son. It was due to the heartbreaking incident where John Jr. heroically attempted to save a woman during a flood but lost his own life in the process. This event, just a few years prior, had visibly taken a toll on John.

By October of 1897, John's health had deteriorated further, confining him to bed for a brief period. His sister, Mrs. Dr. Garcia, took him to St. Louis for specialized care. There, a renowned physician, Dr. Nuboff, diagnosed John's condition as terminal after consulting with other specialists. From that point forward, hope for recovery dwindled. John Connallin's life, marked by both success in business and the profound grief of losing his son, came to an end surrounded by family in St. Louis, where his burial was also made.

The legal entanglements and familial discord that marked John Connallin's life extended even beyond his death. John Connallin was a successful businessman whose substantial estate became the center of a contentious legal struggle following his death. He passed away in Fort Scott, Kansas, leaving behind a fortune that drew the attention of various family members and potential heirs. Connallin's estate included significant property and assets, making it a valuable inheritance.

The main conflict arose around the interpretation of his will. Mary Margaret Connallin, residing in Chicago, launched a legal suit in Fort Scott to claim the entirety of her father's estate. Mary Margaret, the daughter of Georgia Connallin, an actress and singer, asserted her right to the inheritance through the probate court. Her claim suggested she was the rightful heir to her father, John Connallin's wealth.

Mary Margaret's legal action was a direct challenge to the provisions of John Connallin's will, which other family members believed did not support her claim. Specifically, Mrs. Dr. Garcia, a sister from St. Louis, and James Connallin, a brother of the deceased, opposed her suit. They contended that John Connallin's will intended for the estate to be distributed to the next of kin and did not favor the current claimant, implying that Mary Margaret and her mother, Georgia Connallin, were not the intended beneficiaries.

According to his will, John Connallin wrote, "I give and bequeath unto the child Mary Margaret Connallin, (who is not my child, but is the daughter of Georgina Connallin whose maiden name was Georgina Singly, and who was formerly my wife but whom I have been divorced) the sum of ($5.00) Five Dollars."

There was much controversy surrounding his will. However, John Connallin's passing marked the end of an era for his immediate family. His only surviving relatives, his sister Mrs. Garcia and James F. Connallin of Fort Scott laid him to rest in St. Louis. However, twenty years earlier, the Connallin family story took an unexpected turn with the introduction of Charles Garcia, which later intertwined the destinies of the two families – the Connallin and the Garcia family.

Chapter Eight:
Charles Garcia's Legacy

The Connallin family story took an unexpected turn with the introduction of Charles Garcia, which later intertwined the destinies of the two families – the Connallin and the Garcia family.

After the war in 1865, a young Charles, with nothing more than 40 cents to his name, arrived in St. Louis. This tall, strong-looking man with a beard left a lasting impression. Through hard work and perseverance, he managed to save some money. (Death Was Delayed 1889)

Fate intervened when Charles sought out General Dr. Joseph Nash McDowell, a renowned surgeon, as suggested by General P.T. Beauregard. McDowell, perhaps impressed by Charles's determination, took him under his wing. Learning about the reopening of the Missouri Medical College for the 1868-69 session, Charles set his sights on a new goal – becoming a doctor.

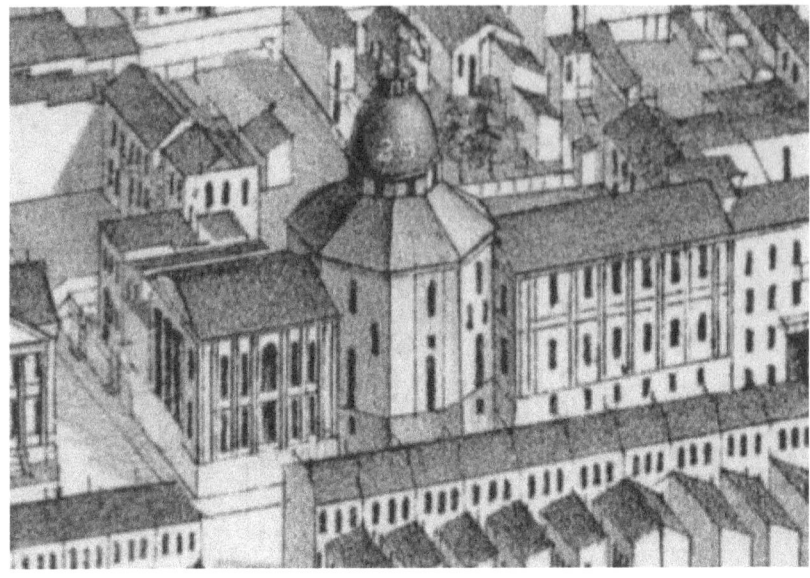

Original McDowell Medical College on Gratiot and 8th, St. Louis, MO. Compton, Richard J., and Camille N. Dry. Pictorial St. Louis, the great metropolis of the Mississippi valley; a topographical survey drawn in perspective A.D. St. Louis: Compton & Co., 1876.

The path to becoming a doctor wasn't cheap. Charles needed $105 for tuition and $45 for additional fees. On top of that, there was the cost of acquiring essential medical textbooks. The list included: PRACTICE OF MEDICINE-Watson, Flint, Hartshorne; MATERIA MEDICA-Wood, Stille, Pereira & Varing; PHYSIOLOGY-Carpenter, Todd & Bowman, Draper, Dalton; CHEMISTRY-Brande & Taylor, Fownc, Graham, Bowman, Fresenius; PHARMACY-Mohr Redwood & Proctor, Parrish, U.S. Dispensatory; OBSTETRICS-Bedford, Cazeaux, Ramsbotham; DISEASES OF WOMEN-Thomas, Hewitt, Sims; DISEASES OF CHILDREN-Condie, Vest; ANATOMY-Gray, Wilson, Holden (Dissector). The syllabus covered a wide range of subjects, from surgery and medicine to anatomy and obstetrics. Interestingly, the passage highlights the fact that germ theory was gaining acceptance in medical practice at this time while anesthesia and intravenous fluids were still in their early stages. (Missouri Medical College 1868)

Charles Garcia's ambition and Dr. Joseph Nash McDowell's mentorship set the stage for a new chapter. Born in Kentucky in 1805, Dr. McDowell earned his medical degree before establishing a medical school in St. Louis in 1839. He brought with him a reputation as a brilliant anatomist and captivating teacher but also as a hothead with a confrontational approach. Public pronouncements often saw him ridicule his adversaries, particularly the Catholics and Jesuits who planned to open a rival medical school.

Dr. McDowell's legacy is a curious mix of innovation and controversy. He constructed a medical school building. The location of this college, now occupied by Ralston Purina, stands as a tangible reminder of a bygone era in St. Louis medicine.

One of the darkest aspects of Dr. McDowell's career involves accusations of body snatching. In an era when cadavers were scarce for medical education, Dr. McDowell was suspected of stealing corpses from local cemeteries for dissection purposes. These suspicions fueled frequent searches of his school and even mob invasions. The reports of Dr. McDowell hiding in chimneys or under dissection tables to avoid capture reflect the fear and outrage he inspired. (Logsdon 2022)

Dr. McDowell's secessionist views further tarnished his reputation. During the Civil War, his medical college was confiscated. While his contributions to medical education in St. Louis were undeniable, his methods and personality were far from exemplary. Ironically, Dr. McDowell's institution eventually merged with others to form the Washington University School of Medicine in 1891. Charles Garcia's decision to study under Dr. McDowell placed him at the center of a fascinating yet turbulent part in St. Louis medical history.

Charles Garcia's journey towards becoming a doctor unfolded over two years. After enrolling in the 1868-1869 session at the Missouri Medical College, he earned his M.D. He extended his studies for an additional year through the 1869-1870 session. During this time, he resided at 7th & Papin St. (Missouri Medical College 1868) (The St. Louis Medical Reporter 1869)

Fate intervened when Charles and Margaret Mary Connallin's (Maggie's) paths crossed. Maggie, the daughter of William and Margaret, was 13 when the family arrived in St. Louis. While a family letter mentions her attending St. Joseph's Academy, there's no record of her enrollment. She likely attended a parochial school connected to the Annunciation of the Blessed Mary Catholic Church near their residence.

As Charles resided at 7th & Papin, love blossomed between Maggie and Charles Garcia. They were married on May 5th, 1869, at the Church of the Annunciation by Rev. P.S. Phelan. Curiously, the ceremony wasn't documented in the church's records or the city's registry. Despite this missing record, a wedding announcement appeared in both the New Orleans Time-Picayune and the Missouri Republican newspapers, even requesting distribution to newspapers in the East. (Married 1869)

Shortly after their wedding, Charles and his wife welcomed their first child, Felix William Garcia, who was born on June 2, 1870. Hearing the joyous announcement, Charles's half-sister, Marie Aimeé Garcia, decided to travel to St. Louis to attend the baptism at the Annunciation of the Blessed Virgin Mary Church. Aimeé had the honor of being named Felix's godmother. The family's happiness was captured forever in a photograph taken at Keller Studios in St. Louis, located on Arsenal at Grand. In this snapshot, Charles and Aimeé stood side by side, their bond evident in their smiles and shared pride.

Charles and Aimée Marie Garcia. Keller Studios, 5551 Arsenal at Grand Ave., St. Louis, MO.

Around the same time, Charles quickly built a successful practice through newspaper advertisements. By April 1874, Dr. Garcia had expanded his practice, hiring a nurse to assist him. With his practice flourishing, a dedicated nurse by his side, and his loving family, things were working out well for Charles Garcia. (Situations Wanted - Females 1874)

In the early days of his career, Charles Garcia operated his medical practice from the Connallins' residence at 406 Cerre St. His exceptional skills and expertise quickly gained attention, and his noteworthy cases were documented in the 1873 St. Louis Medical and Surgical Journal. Dr. Garcia's reports included treating a severe head injury, removing a tumor, and setting fractures using plaster-of-Paris. He also wrote about the proper administration of pain-relieving substances such as opiates, chloroform, Calabar bean, and chloral hydrate. One of his articles described the treatment of a child with a painful mouth condition, where the teeth had turned black, and the gums were sore. Dr. Garcia mentioned using remedies like chlorate of potash, a weak muriatic acid solution, copper sulfate solution, and cinchona powder. Additionally, he shared his experiences in excising cataracts and employing atropine to dilate the eye before surgery. (Hospital Reports 1873)

Dr. Garcia's medical cases were widely reported in the St. Louis Globe-Democrat as well. One notable case involved an infected knee joint that ultimately required amputation due to the worsening infection despite attempts to drain the affected area. Another case involved a brewery worker who had a keg of beer dropped on his foot, resulting in a deep cut to the bone. Dr. Garcia skillfully stitched the wound to promote healing. He also treated a young boy with severe burns on his leg caused by scalding water, set a broken leg resulting from an industrial accident, and performed the removal of a severely damaged eye on a boy who had been struck with a piece of slate.

Additionally, Dr. Garcia treated a non-fatal gunshot wound caused by two boys playing with a pistol and performed an amputation on a hand caught in gears at the Southern White Lead Mills. These cases highlight Dr. Garcia's expertise and dedication to providing quality medical care to his patients. (Joseph L Bauer 1883)

Despite the many triumphs of life, the Garcia family faced some adversities as well. They experienced a setback when thieves attempted to ruin their Christmas in December 1875. That year, Charles's efforts to create a memorable holiday for their sons Felix, Charles, and baby John went in vain. The thieves broke into their residence on 406 Cerre Street, stealing a significant amount of clothing and valuable items. Among the stolen items were a French merino dress adorned with lace, a Scottish plaid dress, a pearl opera-glass, Dr. Garcia's finest attire, including pantaloons, vests, and coats, as well as the brand-new suits of the two boys. (Globe Democrat 1875)

However, Charles Garcia refused to let such incidents dampen his spirits. He continued striving and in 1876, he hired Mrs. E. Grunder and a resident midwife to aid him in his medical practice. The following year, Charles purchased a plot of land at 2500 Carr Street and obtained a permit to construct a new home. The family settled into their new residence, which would be their cherished abode until 1884. The household expanded to include a full-time housekeeper, a hostler responsible for tending to the horses, a couple of boarders, and their growing family of six boys. (Globe Democrat 1880)

Beyond those already mentioned, Dr. Charles Garcia's medical career was marked by a multitude of achievements. He was among the first hospital staff at St. Mary's Infirmary in St. Louis, Missouri. Shortly after the hospital's opening in May 1877, a clinic was established where Dr. Garcia provided free consultations, charging a moderate fee for medicine to those who could afford it while providing medicine free of charge to the poor. (Stueber 2012)

Apart from his medical achievements, the Garcia family was actively involved in the social scene of St. Louis. In their new home on Carr Street, they hosted a captivating lecture by John Graham MaClaine titled "Crossing the Atlantic, or Life Scenes on Shipboard." The event was enhanced by the musical talents of Charles, who played the violin, and his son Felix, who played the cornet. (Globe Democrat 1880)

Additionally, Dr. Garcia served as the treasurer of the Lafayette Association, a civic organization dedicated to promoting the Lafayette Square area of town. The association was formed in February 1881, and Dr. Garcia played an important role in its activities. These accomplishments highlight Dr. Garcia's commitment to his medical practice, his engagement in the community, and his dedication to providing quality healthcare to those in need. (Stueber 2012)

Despite his growing success, Dr. Charles Garcia experienced another unfortunate incident of theft. In 1882, his mare was stolen, and he was involved in a minor buggy accident. The theft occurred in front of the Church of the Holy Angels, prompting Dr. Garcia to offer a $50 reward for the recovery of the stolen rig. Additionally, during the same year, Dr. Garcia and a friend encountered an accident while driving down Gratiot. The buggy struck a streetcar track, causing the rear axle to break and throwing both men to the ground. The frightened horse then ran off, but fortunately, no serious harm was done except to the buggy. (Buggy Accident 1882)

In 1883, Dr. Garcia took a trip to the East Coast, as reported in the Globe-Democrat. The purpose of his trip remains a mystery, as does his request for his wedding announcement to be picked up by Eastern

Papers. Furthermore, in April 1888, he embarked on a trip to the Atlantic coast. (Missouri Daily Democrat 1883)

Dr. Charles Garcia was involved in various practices beyond the medical field. One notable involvement was with the Rainwater Rifles, a civic organization for Confederate veterans led by Major Charles Cicero Rainwater. The group engaged in reenactments of marching drills and organized an annual formal reception, which was known to be a "brilliant affair." (On the River 1888)

In terms of his medical career, Dr. Garcia held a significant position at St. Mary's Infirmary, located at 16th and Papin Streets. He served as the physician and surgeon in charge since the founding of the infirmary. However, this led to a move and the construction of a new home at 1231 Chouteau, at the corner of 13th Street. This new location was more convenient than their previous address on 2500 Carr Street. The construction permit allowed for the building of a three-story home with three attached stores, estimated to cost $13,000. The home also featured an attached stable. Notably, Charles and Maggie assumed a 99-year lease on the underlying land, making the property unique. (Globe Democrat 1884)

Saint Mary's Infirmary has a rich and diverse institutional history. It all began when the Sisters of Saint Mary started searching for suitable locations to establish a small hospital in 1872. Eventually, in 1877, they acquired a former mansion located at 1536 Papin Street, which became the new home for their operation, aptly named Saint Mary's Infirmary. The mansion had a notable history, previously being the residence of Felix Coste, but its most famous former owner was Carl Schurz, who served as a US Senator from Missouri and Secretary of the Interior at various times.

One of Dr. Charles Garcia's early endeavors at St. Mary's Infirmary was the construction of a quarantine facility specifically designed for suspected cases of rabid dogs. This project reflected Dr. Garcia's commitment to the well-being of both human and animal patients.

Charles Garcia. This portrait was last seen at the home of Louise Garcia Lever in Huntleigh, MO. Painted late 1880s.

During his tenure at St. Mary's Infirmary, Dr. Charles Garcia provided care for a significant number of in-patients. Between August 1880 and January 1889, he attended to a total of 930 individuals within the hospital's walls. Additionally, the Sisters of Saint Mary played a crucial role in patient care, extending their nursing services into the homes of patients. During the same period, Dr. Garcia acted as the attending physician for 55 patients in their own residences, further highlighting his dedication to serving the community. (Stueber 2012)

Based on the historical records, it was evident that under the direction of the physicians, the Sisters at Saint Mary's Infirmary became proficient bedside nurses. Recognizing the need for a pharmacy, Mother Odilia ensured that the institution had someone in charge of pharmaceutical duties. At that time, the role of a "druggist" involved tasks such as rolling pills, making extracts and tinctures, and more. While becoming a druggist required taking a course in pharmacy, it did not necessitate a State Board Examination. (Stueber 2012)

Dr. Charles Garcia, a member of the medical staff, offered his services as an instructor, with Sister Mary Aloysia Schruefer as his first student. As the pharmacy became adequately equipped, Sister Mary Aloysia began her work under the supervision of Dr. Garcia. This collaboration between the medical staff and the Sisters highlights their commitment to providing comprehensive care to the patients at Saint Mary's Infirmary.

Unfortunately, in 1888, Charles's health began to deteriorate, likely due to the effects of his service during the war. The unsanitary conditions and filthy train travel experienced as a soldier led to Charles contracting consumption, which is now known as tuberculosis.

To improve his health, Charles decided to escape the hot, humid, and muggy air of St. Louis. In March of 1888, he traveled to Fort Worth, Texas, where he stayed at the Ellis Hotel. He was accompanied by his son Charles on this trip. Later that year, in August, Charles took his son Felix to St. Paul and then embarked on a journey out west to the Pacific. This trip coincided with the opening of Yellowstone Park for visitors, and they may have been attracted to the hot thermal waters there. The train stopped at Livingston, Montana, and from there, they traveled to Mammoth Hot Springs by stagecoach. They continued their journey all the way to the West Coast and back by rail. Additionally, Charles took his son John to New Orleans, where John had the opportunity to meet Marie Aimeé, Charles's half-sister. They stayed at the Cassidy Hotel in New Orleans. In December 1889, Charles once again visited Fort Worth, this time accompanied by his eldest son, Felix. (Ft. Worth Gazette 1888)

Ellis Hotel, Ft. Worth, TX where Charles Garcia passed away. Courtesy of the Fort Worth History Center, Fort Worth Public Library. Amon Carter Photographs. Box 1, Item 5.

These trips to different locations were likely undertaken in the hopes of finding a more favorable climate and environment for Charles's health. It was common during that time for individuals with respiratory conditions like tuberculosis to seek relief in areas with cleaner air and different climates.

However, Dr. Charles Garcia's life, marked by dedication to medicine, culminated in a successful career tragically cut short. At the young age of 45, he passed away in Fort Worth, Texas, at the Ellis Hotel. His remains were brought back to St. Louis by rail, where they lay in repose at the family home on Chouteau Avenue, followed by burial at Calvary Cemetery. His son Felix graduated from medical school at the age of 19. Felix further continued his medical studies in the following years. (Telegram 1889)

Prior to his untimely demise, Dr. Garcia had established himself as a highly skilled and popular physician in St. Louis. He held esteemed positions within the medical community, serving as a member of the Board of Surgeons and the house physician and surgeon of St. Mary's Infirmary since its inception. Dr. Charles Garcia's legacy lived on, not just in the memories of his family but also in the lives he touched through his medical practice.

His obituary was picked up by many newspapers including the run-in with General Bragg. He was survived by six sons, Aimeé Maria Garcia, his half-sister, and his grandmother in Paris. (St. Louis Post Dispatch 1889)

Dr. Charles Garcia's journey, from a young man with little to his name to a respected physician in St. Louis, was marked by both triumph and adversity. Overcoming financial limitations, he built a successful practice, treating a wide range of patients and even venturing into surgery. His story transcends the specifics of his medical practice or personal struggles. It compels us to consider the essence of legacy. Legacy isn't simply about grand gestures or monumental achievements. It's entrenched in the everyday acts of dedication, the pursuit of knowledge, and the unwavering care for others. Dr. Garcia's legacy lives on in the lives he touched, the institution he shaped, and the inspiration he provided for his own son to follow in his footsteps.

Despite the challenges he faced, including illness and theft, Dr. Garcia left a lasting legacy on the medical landscape of St. Louis.

Epilogue

Mrs. Dr. Charles Garcia, affectionately known as Margaret Mary (Maggie) Connallin, faced quite a challenging life after being widowed at the age of 44. Due to her husband's passing, Maggie had to take on the formidable task of raising their six sons alone. The estate left to her was placed in trust for the benefit of their sons' education. This estate included properties on Chouteau, $5,000 in railroad stock, various lots near Springfield, Missouri, cash, and personal items. Maggie diligently collected past-due accounts from her late husband's medical practice to sustain the family financially. She lived in the family home on Chouteau for some time, taking on boarders to make ends meet. Eventually, she moved to South St. Louis on Grand Avenue to live with her eldest son, Felix. Interestingly, the lots in Lawrence County were acquired in payment for medical services rendered by her husband. Unfortunately, these lots were later forfeited to Lawrence County due to non-payment of taxes. Maggie passed away in 1909, leaving behind a legacy of resilience and dedication to her family.

Charles's half-sister, Marie Aimeé Garcia, remained in New Orleans. She was listed as a teacher in the 1900 and 1910 census. She passed away on March 12, 1912. She was said to have been cared for by the Masonic Lodge and may have had a Masonic funeral, but we have no record of it.

Felix William Garcia MD

Felix William Garcia, Maggie's eldest son, became a respected doctor and surgeon in St. Louis. Renowned for his kindness and gentle demeanor, Felix's medical career was distinguished by his commitment to his patients. He maintained an office at 2926 Gravois in St. Louis and practiced at St. Mary's Infirmary and Hospital. Felix was known for providing free medical care to the Little Sisters of the Poor for decades, a reflection of his selfless nature. He attended St. Louis Medical College, which later became part of Washington University, and graduated in 1893. After interning at City Hospital in 1893 and 1894, Felix became a Professor of Abdominal and Pelvic Surgery at The Hippocratean College of Medicine. Prior to this, he served as an Assistant in Anatomy at the Marion-Sims Beaumont College of Medicine.

Felix's contributions to the medical field were significant. He authored several articles on abdominal and pelvic surgery, as well as on the use of medicines in anesthesia, which were published in esteemed journals such as the St. Louis Medical Review and The American Journal of Clinical Medicine. He was an active member and officer of the Missouri State Medical Association and served as a Vice-President of the Tri-State Medical Society of Illinois, Iowa, and Missouri. Outside his medical career, Felix was a member of a Franco-American Club in St. Louis that promoted literature, music, and society. Fluent in French, Felix had a passion for music, evidenced by his performance at a St. Louis University Exhibit in 1888, playing the violin.

In his personal life, Felix married Ida Katherine Pickel on December 21, 1887. Ida's father, John George Pickel, was born in Germany and co-owned a stone and marble company in St. Louis with his brothers. Felix and Ida had five children: Edith, Louise, Adele, Charles, and Virginia. Their son, Charles, named after his grandfather, also became a doctor. Felix was an avid reader, enjoying works by Shakespeare and other great authors, and often read in the evenings after work. He was also fond of smoking cigars, a habit that unfortunately led to cancer of the larynx. Felix passed away on February 11, 1936, at the age of sixty-six, leaving a legacy of compassion and dedication to his patients. (Jost 2014)

Dr. Charles J. Garcia, born in April 1873 in St. Louis, Missouri, pursued a career in dentistry. Despite his professional success, Charles never married and passed away on January 22, 1953. He was laid to rest in Calvary Cemetery in St. Louis.

John Adrian Garcia, PhD, born on August 26, 1875, was the son of Dr. Charles Garcia and Margaret Mary Connallin Garcia. John followed a distinguished academic and professional path, graduating from St. Louis University at the young age of nineteen. In 1900, he earned his Bachelor of Science in Mining Engineering from the School of Mines at the University of Missouri, Rolla. He furthered his education, receiving a Master of Engineering in 1903 and a Doctor of Engineering in 1928. John's professional career began in railroad construction and locations in Missouri, Arkansas, Arizona, and Oklahoma in 1900. His career in mining engineering was notable, with active involvement in the construction, development, and operation of coal mines in the United States, Mexico, and Canada from 1904 to 1908. In 1908, he became chief engineer of the Dering Coal Company, eventually rising to the positions of general superintendent, vice president, and general manager of both the Dering Coal Company and the Brazil Block Coal Company.

In 1911, John became president of the Allen and Garcia Company, which gained international recognition as a specialist in the mining of coal, rock salt, and fluorspar. John continued to lead this distinguished firm of consulting engineers until his death. He married Virginia Mae Seay on September 6, 1902. Virginia was a niece of Governor Seay of

Oklahoma. Together, they had a son, John Adrian Garcia Jr., and a daughter, Virginia Garcia McCarthy. John was a respected member of various engineering societies, including the American Institute of Mining Engineers, the Illinois Mining Institute, the Western Society of Engineers, and the Engineers' Club. He served as president of the Western Society of Engineers in 1928-29 and was also a member of the Tau Beta Pi honorary fraternity. John's life was tragically cut short on August 11, 1939, just before his sixty-fourth birthday, due to a freak accident at home. He was greatly appreciated by everyone who knew him and was regarded as one of the ablest mining engineers in America. (URBANA-CHAMPAIGN 1943)

Dr. Emanuel J. Garcia, born in September 1877, was the second of Maggie and Charles' sons to pursue a career in dentistry. Emanuel, like his brother Charles, never married. He passed away on November 3, 1965, and was buried in Calvary Cemetery, St. Louis.

Dr. Eugene M. Garcia, born in January 1880, was the third dentist in the family. Eugene experienced a tragic accident that profoundly impacted his life. He was driving Miss Ida Schwartz home in a buggy when a shaft broke and struck the horse's leg, causing the animal to bolt. Despite Eugene's efforts to control the horse, Miss Schwartz, in a state of panic, attempted to leap from the buggy. Eugene tried to stop her, but she was hysterical and plunged headlong from the moving vehicle, striking her head on the pavement and fracturing her skull. Dr. Henmerich, a passerby, managed to stop the runaway horse and provided first aid. Eugene was grief-stricken by the incident and vowed never to marry, unable to face the prospect of delivering such devastating news to another family. Eugene passed away on July 2, 1958, and was buried in Calvary Cemetery, St. Louis. (St. Louis Post Dispatch 1905)

Leon Connallin Garica MD

Dr. Leon Connallin Garcia, born on June 12, 1882, made significant contributions to military medicine. As a pioneer in battlefield triage during World War I, Leon was among the first Army medical officers to go to the trenches with soldiers. He served in the Philippines and Mexico before joining the Argonne fighting as chief surgeon of the Sixteenth Infantry Regiment, First Division. Leon's military service earned him several decorations, including the Purple

Heart, the French Medaille d'Honneur, and the Pershing citation. He retired after World War I with the rank of Colonel and practiced medicine in San Francisco. Leon married Marguerite, and they had one child who did not survive. The couple lived in a beautiful home at 114 Santa Paula Avenue in San Francisco. Leon passed away on March 18, 1955, and is buried at San Francisco National Cemetery near the Presidio. (St. Louis Post Dispatch 1955)

The story of the Garcia family is one of resilience, dedication, and remarkable achievements. Maggie Connallin's staunch determination to provide for her sons set the foundation for their future successes. Felix's compassionate medical practice, John's pioneering work in mining engineering, and Leon's groundbreaking contributions to military medicine highlight the diverse and impactful legacies of the Garcia family. Each member faced personal challenges and tragedies, yet their collective story is one of triumph over adversity. Their contributions to their respective fields and communities remain a reflection of their enduring legacy, inspiring future generations to pursue excellence with the same fervor and commitment.

Slave List Inherited by Felix Garcia and Matilde Arnauld

Recorded October 1846, St. John the Baptist Parish, Louisiana Some slaves were owned by daughter Aimée Garcia

Name	Age	Gender	Description
Nathan	28	M	Black American
John	40	M	
Lucille	40	F	
Raymond	36	M	
Lloyd	40	M	
Rachel	50	F	
Adam	27	M	
Laurenz	22	M	
Honore	26	F	
Cheodore	26	M	
Paqui	30	F	
Peteoiu	28	M	Griffe
Camille	28	F	Griffonne
Raymond		M	

Arthemise	23	F	Mulatto
Celeste	27	F	
Marguerite	34	F	
Bebed	10	F	
Louis	7	M	
Joseph	3	M	
Philomine	1	F	
Heloise	48	F	
Ursin	30	F	
Antoine	28	M	
Adelaide	31	F	
Coralie	23	F	
Marianne	42	F	
Celestin	26	M	
Pierre	22	M	
Casimir	18	M	Mulâtre
Clara	13	F	Mulatto
Estelle	7	F	Mulatto
Constance	11	F	

Frosine	24	F	
Claire	47	F	
Sansnom	27	M	Griffe
Francoise	27	F	
De'treville	4	M	Griffe
Victor	6 mos	M	Griffe
Dorothee	30	F	
Pauline	14	F	
Ferdinand	6 mos	M	
Rose	40	F	
Louise	38	F	
Joseph	22	M	
Louis al Bibe	41	M	
Alexis	37	M	
Fox	28	M	
Salomon	28	M	
Daniel	38	M	
James	35	M	
William	49	M	Mulâtre

Celestine	6	F	
Joseph	3	M	
Joafsina	1	F	
Cherise	28	F	
Manette	4	F	
Auguste	2 mos	M	
Marie	35	F	
Augustine	10	F	
Baptiste	6	M	
Francois	4	M	
Eulalie	17	F	Griffonne
Bufsin	44	M	
Peter	41	M	
Dick	31	M	
Chiso	45	M	
Baker	40	M	
Es Charley	38	M	
Ferdinand	31	M	
Jean	33	M	

Com	23	M	
Bill	23	M	
Lucile	37	F	
Rachel	43	F	
Lucile Joe	33	F	
Lucile Martin	31	F	
Hanny	33	F	
Pheobe	35	F	
Morffy or Mory	29	F	
Eugene	4	M	
Mary	1	F	
Charlotte	26	F	
Jean	5	M	
Valcort	1	M	
Albert	43	M	
Achille	44	M	
Borel	36	M	Mulatto
Lewis	40	M	
Marelle	38	M	

Andrew Jackson	42	M	
Euta	42	M	
Rasumus	40+	M	Griffe
Charlos	36	M	
Washington	41	M	
Moses	43	M	
Fran----	29	F	Mulâtresse
Patrice	38	F	
Sam Moutz	42	M	
Daniel	31	M	
Field	34	M	
Cho----	36	M	
Petit Henry	19	M	
------	32	M	
Gueri Braia	40+	M	
Big Henry	36	M	
Jasmin	44	F	
Jacques Baumond	34	M	

Sam	34	M	
Jean	36	M	Mulâtre
Jacques Davis	44	M	
Hilaire	17	F	
Henry Verreh	34	M	
Francois	27	M	
Peter	42	M	
Bob	29	M	
William		M	
John Mack	30	M	
Grand John	29	M	
Isaac	31	M	
Kerry	20	M	
William	14	M	
Hanny Brown	32	F	
Marie Jeanne	28	F	
Betsey	33	F	Mulâtresse
Henriette	14	F	Mulâtresse
Lisa	12	F	

Frank	9	M	
Clarifse	6	F	
Prosper	3	M	Mulâtre
Paul	1	M	Mulatto
Anna	26	F	
Louisa	16	F	
Adolphe	6	M	
Elizabeth	4	F	
Caroline	1	F	
Louisa	26	F	
August	10	M	
Marianne	8	F	
----	6		
Letty	36	F	
----	14	F	
Lucile	9	F	
Celeste	8	F	
Celestine	8	F	
Melite	6	F	

Juliette	4	F	
Rosalie	28	F	
Celeste	3	F	
Goe	10+	F	
Octavie	6	F	Mulâtre

Works Cited

"Arrived Jackson." Mobile Register (Mobile, AL), March 13, 1862.

"Beauregard Rifles." Times-Picayune (New Orleans, LA), sec. Classifieds, April 26, 1861.

"Classified Ad 2." Daily Picayune (New Orleans, LA), sec. Military, March 2, 1862.

"Classified Ad 2." Daily Picayune (New Orleans, LA), sec. Military News, March 1, 1862.

"Confederate Louisiana Troops." Revision 12/30/12, National Park Service, http://www.nps.gov/civilwar.

"Crescent Regiment, Attention." Daily Picayune (New Orleans, LA), sec. Military Notices, n.d.

"Editorial Article 3." Daily Picayune (New Orleans, LA), sec. Military Notices, March 5, 1862.

"Follow, Boys! Follow!" Daily True Delta (New Orleans, LA), March 8, 1862.

"Honors To Col B. Frank Terry." Daily Picayune (New Orleans, LA), December 23, 1861.

"Interesting Presentation Ceremonies." The Daily Picayune (New Orleans, LA), sec. Editorial Article 2, November 16, 1861.

"Military Notices." Times-Picayune (New Orleans), February 2, 1862.

"Off For The Seat Of War." Daily Picayune (New Orleans, LA), sec. Editorial Article 3, March 9, 1862.

"Ordered Shot: Dr. Charles Garcia's Experience At The Wrong End Of A Musket." St. Louis Post Dispatch (St. Louis, MO), sec. Page 2, July 7, 1887.

"Our Army At Corinth." Charleston Mercury (Charleston, SC), sec. News of the War, April 4, 1862.

"The City." Daily Picayune (New Orleans, LA), sec. The City, March 4, 1862.

"The Crescent Regiment." Daily Picayune (New Orleans, LA), sec. Front Page, December 2, 1861.

"The Crescent Regiment." Daily True Delta (New Orleans, LA), March 7, 1862.

"The Crescent Regiment." Trenton State Gazette (Trenton, NJ), June 28, 1865.

"The Reception Of Gen. Twigg." Daily Picayune (New Orleans, LA), sec. The City, March 6, 1861.

"The Recruiting Service." Daily Picayune (New Orleans, LA), sec. The City, April 20, 1861.

"Uniforms." Daily Delta (New Orleans, LA), March 9, 1862.

"Washington Artillery And Crescents En Route." Times-Picayune (New Orleans, LA), March 11, 1862.

"We Are Requested." Daily Picayune (New Orleans, LA), sec. Editorial Article 2, March 27, 1862.

"Beauregard Rifles." Times-Picayune (New Orleans, LA), sec. The City, April 18, 1861.

Americus (GA) Recorder. "He Was A Brave Fellow." Kansas City Times (Kansas City, MO), June 28, 1887.

John Skardon. Facebook discussion with Daniel Oppliger, Surprise, AZ, January 11, 2013.

Sparta. "From The Seat Of War." Daily Picayune (New Orleans, LA), sec. Special Correspondence, March 28, 1862.

Alpha Register Montmartre. 1859. "Alpha Register Montmartre." Alpha Register Montmartre.

Ames, Richard. 2015. "Manuel Garcia Report." Pensacola, FL: University of West Florida.

Blanc, Terence Le. 1842. "Mortgage Recording." New Orleans, June 20.

Carlos Garcia vs Felix Garcia and Dunlop Moncure & Company. 1852. 7 La Ann 525 (Supreme Court of Louisiana, St. Paul June).

Charity Hospital. 1852. "Patient Records." New Orleans: Charity Hospital, December 20.

Christophe Strantz. 1850. 20885034 (4th Judicial District Court of Louisiana Parish of St. John the Baptist, February 15).

Creative Media Partner, LLC. 2022. Report of the Special Committee on the Mexican Gulf Railroad. Creative Media Partners, LLC.

Daily Advocate. 1859. "Louisiana Legislature." Daily Advocate.

Daily Atlas. 1845. "Garcia Shot." Daily Atlas, May 12.

Daily Delta. 1857. "A Duel." November 16.

Daily Missouri Democrat. 1874. "Situations Wanted - Females." April 22.

Daily Missouri Republican. 1869. "Married." May 10.

Daily Picayune. 1847. "Praiseworthy Conduct." Daily Picayune, September 23.

—. 1891. "Weather and Crops." Daily Picayune, June 21.

Daily Picayune. 1892. "Garcia on Trial." Daily Picayune 3.

De Bow's Review. 1866. De Bow's Review. New Orleans: J.D.B. De Bow.

Democrat Advocate. 1847. "Tribute of Respect to Mr. Felix Garcia." Democrat Advocate, October 6: 2.

Democrat Advocate. 1847. "Grand Celebration." November 10: 2.

Dupotet, Jules. 1853. "Feast Mesmerien of New Orleans." Journal du Magnetisme 12.

Enquirer. 1848. "Singular But Glorious Result." February 4: 4.

Flake's Bulletin. 1868. "The Warfare of the St. Louis Police on Gambling Houses." Flake's Bulletin, March 13.

Ft. Scott Daily Monitor. 1898. "The End Came." Ft. Scott Daily Monitor, March 10.

Ft. Worth Gazette. 1888. "Hotel Arrivals." Ft. Worth Gazette, September 13.

Gandolfo, Jerry. 2014. "Massicot Family of the Cote des Allemands, Louisiana." New Orleans.

Garcia, Virginia May Seay. 1954. "Frames and Photographs." November 5.

Gayarre, Charles. 1866. History of Louisiana, The American Domination. New Orleans.

Ghent University. 1858. "Revue Trimestrielle." Item notes: v 5.

Globe Democrat. 1882. "Buggy Accident." June 17.

Globe Democrat. 1880. "Lecture at Dr. Garcia's Home." Globe Democrat, May 29.

—. 1875. "Physician's House Raided." Globe Democrat, December 22.

—. 1884. "Realty and Building." Globe Democrat, August 16.

—. 1880. "Wanted." Globe Democrat, June 3.

Government Printing Office. 1896. The Department of the Interior and General Land Office in Cases Related to Public Lands. Edited by S.V. Proudfit. Vol. XXII. Washington: Government Printing Office.

"Guadeloupe Privateers in Barataria." The Louisiana Historical Quarterly 23: 429.

History of New Orleans Drainage. New Orleans, LA. https://web.archive.org/web/20060503054649/http://www.mvn.usace.army.mil/pao/history/NO_Drainage/NO_Drain_chap3.pdf.

Holmes, Jack D. L. 1940. Honor and Fidelity. Birmingham: Louisiana Collection Series.

Holmes, Jack D.L. 1965. "Dramatis Personae." Louisiana Historical Quarterly.

Holmes, Jack D.L. 1970. "Pensacola Settlers, 1781-1821." (Pensacola Historical Restoration and Preservation Commission).

"Hospital Reports." Saint Louis Medical and Surgical Journal (E.F. Hobart & CO) 10.

Joseph L. Bauer, MD. 1883. "Clinical Cases." Medical Brief, A Monthly Journal of Practical Medicine, March.

Jost, Marcella. 2014. Felix Alexander Jost. Charlottesville, VA: Unpublished manuscript.

Kotlawī, Abū Yusuf Muḥammad Sharīf Muḥaddiš. n.d. Akhlāq-uṣ-Ṣāliḥīn. Karachi: Maktaba-tul-Madīnah.

La Presse. 1859. "Deces et inhumations." La Presse, January 13.

Le Courrier de la Louisiane. 1849. May 18.

Logsdon, Stephen. 2022. Joseph Nash McDowell The Legend. Prod. Becker Medical Library. St. Louis, MO, February 10. Accessed July 22, 2024. https://becker.wustl.edu/news/joseph-nash-mcdowell-the-st-louis-legend/.

Missouri Daily Democrat. 1883. "Personal." Missouri Daily Democrat, August 26.

Missouri Medical College. 1868. "Annual Announcement." Annual Announcement and Catalogue of the Missouri Medical College. St. Louis, MO: P.M. Pinckard.

Nasatir, Abraham Phineas. 1968. Spanish War Vessels on the Mississippi, 1792-1796. United Kingdom: Yale University Press.

New Orleans Bee. 1884. March 12.

New Orleans Bee. 1852. "Louise Matilde Garcia." New Orleans Bee, September 3.

—. 1849. "Sugar House Fire." New Orleans Bee, March 10.

New York Daily Times. 1853. "Letter from Havana." December 20.

O'Dell, Edith, interview by Daniel Oppliger. 1970.

Orleans, Archdiocese of New. 1803. Sacramental Records. New Orleans: Archdiocese of New Orleans.

Peters, Richard. 1838. Cases Argued and Adjudged in the Supreme Court of the United States. Philadelphia: Thomas, Cowperthwait & Co.

Provost Marshal. 1865. 02-03-1865 F 1468 (Feb 2).

Reed, Merl Elwyn. 1966. New Orleans and the Railroads: The Struggle for Commercial Empire, 1830-1860. Louisiana State University Press.

Rogers, Ashley, interview by Daniel Oppliger. 2020. Hill Memorial Library at LSU in Baton Rouge (June 24).

Sorapuru, Adolphe. 1870. Memoirs of Adolphe Sorapuru. Edited by Marlene Darensbourg. St. John Parish, LA: Unpublished manuscript.

St. Charles Parish. 1807. "St. Charles Original Acts 1807." In St. Charles Original Acts 1807, 50-52. Hahnville, LA.

St. Louis Globe Democrat. 1882. "In a Bad Plight." November 9: 3.

St. Louis Post Dispatch. 1889. "Death Was Delayed." December 10.

St. Louis Post Dispatch. 1889. "Death Was Delayed." St. Louis Post Dispatch, December 10.

—. 1855. "Dr. Leon C. Garcia Dies, Retired Army Surgeon." St. Louis Post Dispatch, March 19.

—. 1905. "Frightened Woman's Jump Causes Death." St. Louis Post Dispatch, September 25.

St. Louis Republic. 1888. "On the River." August 12.

Stueber, Sr. Marylu, interview by Daniel Oppliger. 2012. Franciscan Sisters of Mary.

Telegram, Ft. Worth. 1889. "Dr. Charles Garcia." Ft. Worth Telegram, December 8.

The Daily Picayune. 1844. "Brief Biographical Sketches." The Daily Picayune, September 5: 2.

The Evening Star. 1882. "Bigamous Bouscaren." The Evening Star, September 7.

The St. Louis Medical Reporter. 1869. "Editorial." The St. Louis Medical Reporter, March 1: 118.

Times Picayune. 1848. "Louisiana Legislature." Times Picayune, January 25.

—. 1850. "The Crevasse Above New Orleans." Times Picayune, January 7.

Topeka Weekly. 1891. "The Body of a Brave Rescuer Recovered." Topeka Weekly, July 2.

URBANA-CHAMPAIGN, LIBRARY OF THE UNIVERSITY OF ILLINOIS AT. 1943. Historical encyclopedia of Illinois with commemorative biographies. Vol. III. Edited by WILLIAM P. MUNSELL. Comp. WILLIAM P. MUNSELL. Urbana-Champaign, IL. https://archive.org/stream/historicalen03bate/historicalen03bate_djvu.txt.

US Census. 1880. US Census. Kansas City: US Government Printing Office.

"Wedding Certificate." Marriage Book 3. Edgard, LA: St. John the Baptist Church, February 15.

Weekly Messenger. 1830. "Sugar House Fire." March 11.

Ximenez, Carlos. 1790. "Carlos Ximenez Notarial Acts." New Orleans.

Yoes III, Henry E. 2005. Louisiana's German Coast. Lake Charles, LA: Racing Pigeon Digest Publishing Co.

Zeringue, Earlene, trans. 1828-1840. St. John The Baptist Church Fifth Book of Baptisms. Vol. XIII. Edgard, LA.

Index